# Low Co
# PC Networ    g

# Low Cost
# PC Networking

Mike James

**HEINEMANN**
NEW·TECH

Heinemann Professional Publishing
Halley Court, Jordan Hill, Oxford OX2 8EJ

OXFORD  LONDON  MELBOURNE  AUCKLAND

First published 1989
© M. James

British Library Cataloguing in Publication Data

James, Mike. (Mike)
Low Cost PC Networking
I. Microcomputer systems. Networks
I. Title
004.6


ISBN 0 434 90897 5

Typeset by TypeAce, Ringwood, Hampshire
Printed and bound in Great Britain by
Anchor Press Ltd, Tiptree, Essex

Front cover photograph shows an IBM Personal System/2
with an IBM 8514 colour display showing IBM
Operating System/2 Presentation Manager images.

# Contents

Preface

**Chapter 1    Introduction to low cost LANs**                   9

The grand view – sharing hardware – office communications –
the network in the company – alternatives to networking –
summary

**Chapter 2    Hardware for low cost PC networking**            27

How far? How fast? How many? – bus networks – network
adapters – cabling – other types of network – reflections – physical
details of cabling – summary

**Chapter 3    Software for low cost PC networking**            53

Servers and requesters – power – network types – log on and log off
– requester functions – network names – types of server – device
servers – communications servers – summary

**Chapter 4    Single user applications**                      83

Sharing files – semaphores – the deadly embrace – directory locking
– MS-DOS 3.x and locking – sharing READ-ONLY files –
problems with single user software – explicit locking – shared
programs but private data – MS-DOS 3.x programs – extended
locking – software licences – running real single user products –
summary

**Chapter 5    Multi-user software**                                    *109*

Standards – MS-DOS V3.x and NETBIOS – concurrency,
integrity and consistency – records and byte range locking – single
user databases on a network – high concurrency – the need for file
locks – database servers – when things go wrong – some real
databases – multi-user high level languages – network applications?
– summary


**Chapter 6    Some real products**                                     *129*

IBM's LAN – Apricot networks – Corvus, the Amstrad network –
3Com – Novell – MAPNET – D-Link – D-Link V4 – LANsmart –
SageNet – ZeroNet or Knowledge Net II – DRNet – Torus
Tapestry – Conclusion


**Chapter 7    Planning a network**                                     *177*

Needs, why network? – network = mainframe – system selection –
planning a network – network installation – configuring the
network – network administration – two case studies – conclusion –
summary


**Chapter 8    Future networks**                                        *201*

OS/2 the big change – the OS/2 LAN manager – applications
servers and distributed applications – connecting to mainframes –
internetworking – the MAC, Appletalk – MAP and TOP –
networks in education – summary


**Appendix A    Network technicalities**                                *217*

**Appendix B    Suppliers and contacts**                                *239*

# Preface

The availability of low cost, reliable and capable, networking products for PCs is the single most important event since the introduction of the personal computer over ten years ago. Even in those early days of the Cromemco, Altair and the Commodore PET business users were talking about ways of connecting computers together. The potential of a network of personal computers to be greater than the sum of its parts has always been fairly clear and this has driven manufacturers to introduce networks before their time. The difficulty of building a powerful, reliable and low cost network has always been underestimated and a succession of products that have missed the target have tended to make users suspicious of networks. Every year has been claimed as the 'year of the network' by someone but at last the technology seems to have matured and now is the time to discover what a network could do for you.

This book describes practical networking for the PC user. Many books on networking start by describing only the technology and it is all too easy to become excited about the ideas of networking and forget that there are real products. The theory of networking is now well established and it is time to move on from discussing vague possibilities for the future and deal with the problems and benefits of the existing technology. Many network experts express the unity that a network brings to disparate PCs by saying that "the network is the computer". In my opinion this over-emphasises the importance of the hardware. It is not so much what the network is but more what it will do for you that is important. A network has the potential to draw together all of the operations of your enterprise and in this sense the "the network is the company" is a better motto.

I would like to thank the following companies for their help by way of loaning equipment or providing information: Ahmos Computer Centre, Applied Knowledge Ltd., Apricot Computers plc, Corvus Systems Ltd., Data Translation Ltd., Digital Research, Intelligent Micro Software, Novell Ltd., SageSoft plc, Torus Systems Ltd., Western Digital Ltd., 3-Com Ltd.

# *1.* Introduction to Low Cost LAN's

Networking or **LAN**, Local Area Networking, is simply the connecting together of a number of computers so that they can share data and peripherals. It sounds an easy thing to do but in practice it turns out to be full of potential problems. Indeed it is an area of computing where it is easier to make a mistake than a good investment.

If this makes you think that networking is something to avoid then think again because it is the single most important advance in the way that we use computers since the introduction of the personal computer some ten years ago. You could almost say that the personal computer doesn't make very much sense without networking and networks are a natural stage in their development. If you have a room full of separate PCs then each person has a tool to do a individual task. The use of the PC in this way is a natural extension of the desktop calculator or adding machine – an aid in doing a traditional job in a traditional way. However when you add the extra dimension of networking, the room full of PCs becomes part of the total functioning of the office or training centre. You can think of this as a single isolated PC being a help with the functions of what would normally happen on a single desk whereas the network is an office-wide machine integrating all the functions on all the desks into a single endeavour.

# THE GRAND VIEW

To buy a few PCs you only have to take a small scale or micro view of the functions that your organisation performs. For example, you could buy a PC to help an office junior prepare and maintain a mailing list operation, another to help your accounts clerk run a spreadsheet to keep track of VAT and yet another to help your secretary prepare correspondence. Each of these decisions could be, and usually are, made in isolation. Each machine would be justified on how much it helped its user to complete their allotted task within the company.

As a network is a company-wide system to fully understand its implications you have to take a larger scale view. For example, if one user creates a customer mailing list then it could be of use to the accounts clerk in mailing invoices and reminders or indeed to anyone dealing directly with the firm's customers. In other words, there is a need to think about the way data is created and how it can best be shared and utilised by the rest of the network.

It is often said that the main benefit of a network is the sharing of expensive hardware such as printers. While this is very true the greatest potential benefit comes from the sharing of DATA.

If the prospect of having to organise your computer system on a company-wide scale for the first time sounds like too big and too risky to contemplate then it is worth pointing out that not everything has to be done at once. Most companies will already have a number of isolated PCs and the cost of networking them together is relatively small. Even if there are no changes to the way people have been using their PCs there is already the immediate advantage of being able to share peripherals, such as hard disk drives and printers. This will increase efficiency if only because every computer is now as powerful as the most powerful on the network. In addition there will also be a tendency towards ad-hoc

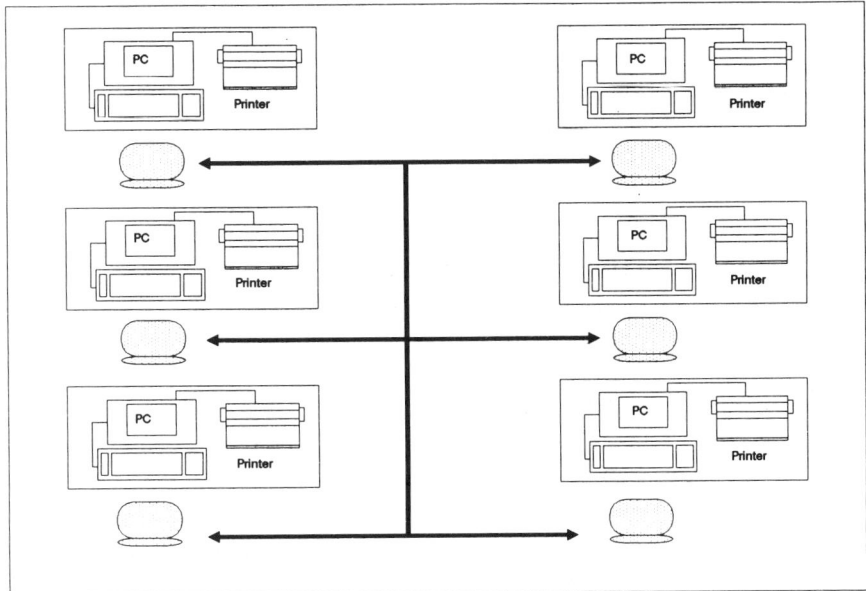

In an office without a network data sharing and
communication is via people

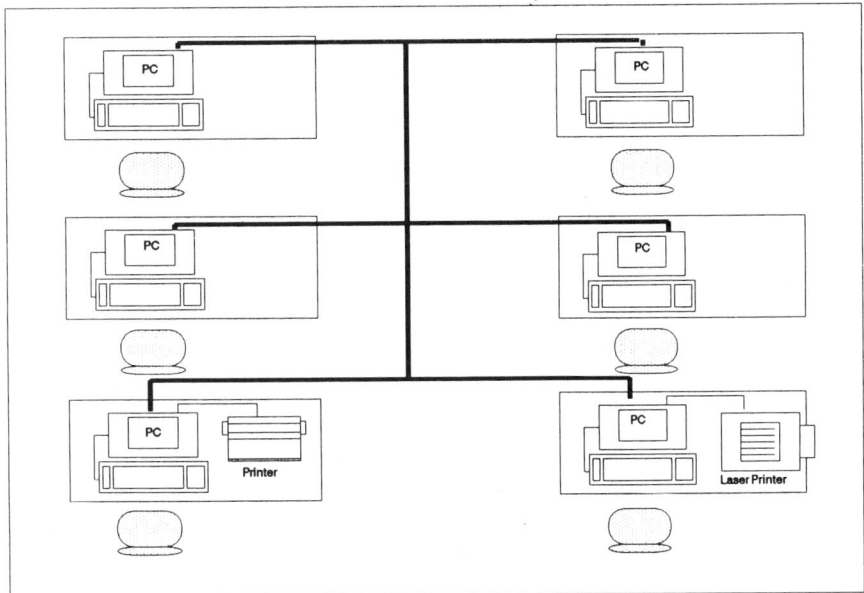

In a networked office the data sharing and
much of the communication is via PCs

11

sharing of data between different users that will highlight what sort of changes should be made to the way everyone works. In other words, there is very little to lose by installing a suitable network as an upgrade to an existing set of PCs.

## SHARING HARDWARE

Although many of the real advantages of installing a network cannot be summarised in terms of just improved computer facilities there are indeed many such advantages to be gained from a network. In the remainder of this chapter we examine the potential hardware benefits of installing a network. Put simply these advantages all stem from being able to share items of hardware but why should this be necessary?

## HARD DISKS

Most networks will allow you to share disk drives. Some will allow you to share any sort of disk drive over the network but in practice, apart from one or two special cases, there is no point in sharing anything other than a hard disk. A hard disk is a high capacity high-speed disk drive. Typical storage capacities are 10, 20 or 30 Mbytes. To give you some idea of how big this capacity is, 30 Mbytes is roughly equivalent to 100 standard (360K) floppy diskettes.

Even though this is a great deal of storage it is not the only reason to prefer a hard disk. If you have only used a PC with floppy disks then it is difficult to appreciate how much easier a hard disk makes using a computer. Usually all of the standard applications programs that you might want to use can be stored on a single hard disk. This means that you can start word-processing or spreadsheet applications without having to look for or keep separate floppies for each.

## Four PCs each with a hard disk

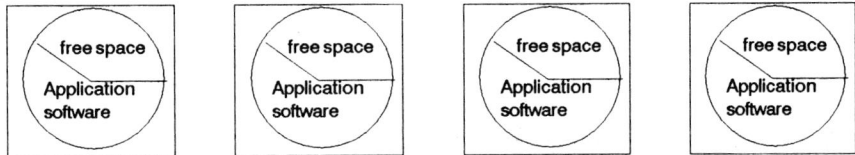

free space

Application software

free space

Application software

free space

Application software

free space

Application software

## Four computers
## sharing one hard disk drive

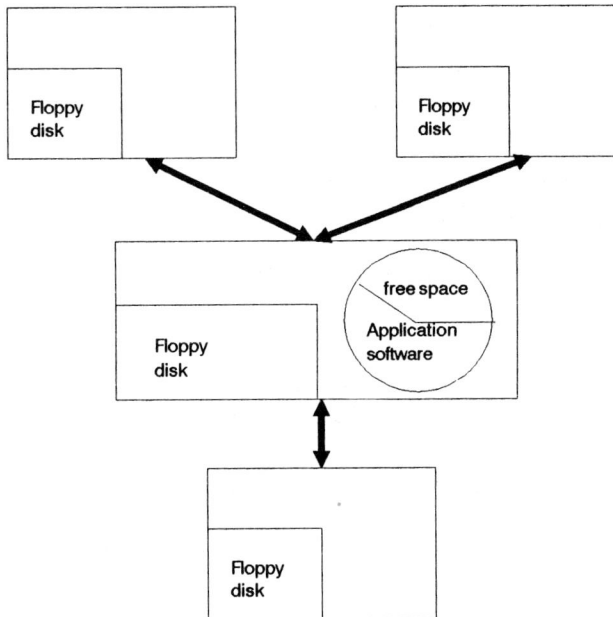

Floppy disk

Floppy disk

Floppy disk

free space

Application software

Floppy disk

In addition a hard disk works some ten times faster than a floppy and this means that applications programs load virtually instantaneously, compared to the clunking of a floppy. Indeed so great are the benefits of a hard disk that many of the best applications programs are designed to work from one and really only give of their best when used from one.

You should be able to see why a hard disk is generally considered to be the minimum requirement for a professional PC. Hard disks do cost more than a floppy but even so the economies of sharing a hard disk over a network seem counter-productive. Surely ten people sharing a 20 Mbyte hard disk reduces the storage for each user down to 2 Mbytes each which is getting close the capacities offered by floppy disks? The answer to this question is no. The reason is that, apart from a few exceptions, the largest files stored on a hard disk are the applications programs. Usually 10 to 15 Mbytes of any hard disk will be used to store applications programs and this reduces the apparent benefit of providing individual drives. Storing multiple copies of an application program doesn't seem like a good use of expensive hard disk drives! A single hard disk can be used over a network to provide access to all of the applications programs used by a company at more or less the same speed and convenience of an individual hard disk. This sharing of applications programs is one of the major advantages of a network and represents a significant improvement in hardware utilisation.

If a single shared hard disk can provide almost the same range of benefits as individual hard disks what additional disk drives, if any, are required at each PC? You can go the whole way and use PCs that have no additional disk drives – so called **diskless workstations** but there are distinct advantages if each PC has a single floppy disk drive. The reason for this probably being the optimum is that while the shared hard disk can be used to supply the applications programs, the single floppy disk can be used to store individual data files. If each user on the network is given the responsibility of looking after their own data files on floppy disk then it simplifies the management of the shared resources. It is quite possible for each user to save data files on the shared hard disk but in practice this generally leads to a full shared hard disk no matter what its capacity is! There are of course some data files that need to be shared and these should most certainly be stored on the shared hard disk but equally files that do not need to be shared should be stored on private devices.

If one floppy disk per workstation is a good investment then why not two? The answer to this is quite simply that once you have access to a hard disk to supply applications programs and a single floppy disk to save data, a second floppy disk spends most of its time idle. A second floppy does no harm but it isn't a great benefit either.

# PRINTERS

A high quality or high speed printer can cost as much as a PC and this clearly makes it uneconomical to provide one per machine. The usual compromise in a non-networked environment is to have one or two high quality printers and a number of cheaper models. A common problem with this arrangement is simply that each type of printer is usually in the wrong place. Also physically moving printers around is possible but generally not good for the printers, nor the users! The network solution to the problem is to plan the overall printing requirements and then buy and share printers that meet these. This doesn't mean that existing printers have no place in a network; they can still provide additional local printing facilities.

The best quality and fastest printers available at the moment are laser printers. These work in the same way as a photocopier only instead of copying an original the computer paints a pattern of dots using a laser on the printing drum. Apart from this change, managing a laser printer is similar to running a photocopier and involves adding toner and changing drums. (Some printers use a single cartridge that contains toner and a new drum.) The resolution of a laser printer is typically 300 by 300 dots per inch and this is good enough to produce near typeset quality output. The printing speed is generally in the range of 6 to 8 pages per minute and typical costs are in the range £1000 to £3000. To provide each PC with an individual laser printer clearly isn't an economical proposition because in most applications a single user cannot keep a laser printer gainfully employed. Of course a shared laser printer not only reduces the cost per user it also increases its utilisation.

You may be wondering how a single printer can be shared between a number of users. Surely if more than one person tries to print at the same time then the different outputs would be printed jumbled together? In practice there are two approaches to the problem of sharing a printer so that this sort of accident doesn't happen. Some networks implement a resource locking scheme that only allows one user at a time to be printing. In this case if a second user tries to print at the same time they receive a polite message to the effect that the printer is busy and they should try again later. This is a simple, if often inconvenient scheme, as it only takes one user printing a long document to lock out all the other users for some time. It is also a fact that in many offices there is a peak time for printer demand – just before the post goes! However the locking system can work well if there are a number of alternative printers shared over a network. Then the user can avoid waiting by looking around to find an unused printer.

The second approach is to implement **printer spooling**. In this case the machine that the printer is actually connected to is designated the **printer server** and collects any printing tasks sent to it in disk files. It then sends each completed print file in turn to the printer. This means that a queue of print files is created, no user has to wait to print something and the printer is kept as busy as possible. Of course the disadvantage is that a print file may not be printed immediately and the user has to wait until the printer has processed print requests that were received earlier. A partial solution to this problem is to allocate priorities to the print files in the queue but even then it still takes longer for output to appear on a spooled printer than on one that is driven directly.

In most cases the ideal configuration is to have a number of shareable printers connected to the network so that any user can choose the printer most suitable or even most available. For example, a wide carriage dot matrix printer is very useful for printing large spreadsheets, a high speed draft printer can be useful for interim prints of documents and so on. There is one point that is often overlooked in planning the printer allocation on a network and that is the need for a hard disk to implement printer spooling. Clearly as printer spooling works by collecting output into disk files the efficiency of the whole operation depends on the speed of the disk drive and in practice this means that you have to use a hard disk drive. Some networks make spooling dependent on the existence of a hard disk others merely advise that one is a good idea. Direct connection to a printer on the other hand generally doesn't need a hard disk. What this means for planning a network is that your most used printers should be connected to hard disk machines.

## OTHER DEVICES

Most networks are designed to allow users to share disk drives and printers and other devices are often added as an afterthought. Indeed some networks will not allow any other resources to be shared over the network. How important such a restriction is depends on what other devices you have connected to your system that you might want to share. Just having a device in a system doesn't mean that it necessarily has to be offered for sharing.

One important class of device that many networks do not allow you to share is **tape drives**. These are mainly used to backup the data on your hard disk so that you can use the copy to restore your data following a system failure. Of course sharing a tape drive only becomes an issue if there is more than one hard disk on the network. Even then there are ways of avoiding sharing the tape drive in order to backup a disk on another machine. (You can simply connect to the remote disk from the workstation that owns the tape drive and run the backup program without sharing the tape drive.)

The only other common types of device that do not fit into either the disk drive or the printer categories are serial devices. Serial devices are a group of peripherals that are connected to a PC via the serial port rather than the more usual parallel or printer port. In terms of the network therefore the issue is more how serial ports can be shared than how any particular type of device can be shared.

Many networks do allow you to share a serial port but only as an alternative form of printer port. That is, you inform the system that you are using a serial rather than parallel printer, and from that moment on spooled output goes to the serial port rather than to the more usual parallel port. This method of sharing is fine for serial printers and plotters but not workable for two-way devices such as modems.

The use of printer spooling to a serial port restricts the flow of information to one direction – from the machine to the external device. A modem or any other communications device needs to send and receive data. In this case only some form of direct sharing will do. Some networks do provide this capability and in principle this could be used to share a single modem over the network. Most communications programs, however, are not very well behaved in the sense that they break the rules and access the hardware directly rather than via the operating system and therefore tend not to work over a network.

# OFFICE COMMUNICATIONS

Having all the PCs in an office connected together by a network also brings with it the possibility of using the network as an extra method of communication. The idea of using electronic mail or **E-mail** within a single office as a way of avoiding paper is attractive but it has to be approached with care. Nearly all networks provide some method of one user sending another user a message. At its most primitive this consists of a single line message that will be delivered as long as the PC that is the destination of the message is switched on. If the PC is not connected then the message is not delivered and in this form the E-mail is an immediate form of communication between users of the network. In a sense it is a network equivalent of a telephone call or an informal talk.

A slightly more sophisticated system uses a central post box PC or **mail server** that is assumed to be always switched on and connected to the network. The mail server collects the E-mail and then sends it out to the intended recipient. If the recipient is not connected to the network at that particular moment then the E-mail is saved until they do switch on and connect. This version of E-mail using a mail server is clearly the most useful in that it is the network equivalent of traditional memos and notes. Indeed some network systems provide onscreen E-mail forms that mimic telephone memos, etc.

The main trouble with the office communication aspect of networking is that it is all too easy to overestimate its value. In a small office people tend to prefer face to face conversations to immediate E-mail communication. Even in a large office paper memos tend to be easier to use and less formal than a full E-mail system. This is not to say that an E-mail system isn't useful but don't expect it to reduce or eliminate the more traditional paper-based communication system that every office uses. It is better to see it as an alternative or additional channel of communication that suits some forms of information better than others.

There is one special form of communication that is especially suited to training situations. Some network systems allow you to examine, and even take over, the screen of another user's PC. The roll that this could play in a computer-based training system is obvious. Perhaps the best simile is that of the language lab where the tutor can listen in and talk to any student.

## THE NETWORK IN THE COMPANY

Although networks do bring many advantages in terms of sharing devices and electronic messaging, a network that is only being used for these things isn't really fulfilling its true potential. A network in this form is simply a collection of PCs that just happen to be thrown together. You wouldn't expect to take a group of people off the street, put them behind desks in a room and expect them to work co-operatively without organisation and the same is true of networked PCs.

Before the network each PC will have been used for some specific task depending on who used it. If you just add a network then the specific uses of each PC will continue but the individual users will start to exchange information on an ad-hoc basis. For example, it might be that before networking a PC was used to keep a spreadsheet for VAT accounting, another was used to create and print invoices and yet another to control stock using a special database program. If a network is installed and no other changes are made you will find that each PC will continue to be used in much the same way. The particular applications programs may now come from a central machine which also supplies printing facilities but each user will stick to their chosen application package and method of working. Over time one or two users might discover that they can communicate with other departments by sending E-mails or by sharing data in files. Of course the problem with sharing data in this way is that each user will probably be using a different type of applications package – for example accounts using a spreadsheet and dispatch using a database. In this instance how can dispatch send information to accounts concerning stock orders and sales? To make the best use of a network's data sharing abilities it is important that different departments use either the same applications program or at least compatible applications programs. Generally this means selecting and adopting a database program that can be used on a network. The reason why this company-wide program is usually a database is that only a database can deal with the record of a transaction from its initiation to its completion and also produce summaries of past transactions. For example, a salesman can create a sales record which gives rise to an invoice to accounts and a packing note to dispatch. The packing note is used by dispatch to update the stock control records. The stock control records are used automatically to place orders for new stock as soon as pre-set re-order levels are reached. These orders can be passed on to accounts so that the purchase part of the VAT accounts can be constructed and so on. From this description it should be clear that the movement of data records around the network, the triggering of actions based upon them, and the preparation of summaries and reports constitutes the necessary flow and use of information that makes a company work. In this sense a well designed network of PCs is the company.

If this idea of a network becoming so central to the operation of your company is worrying it is worth pointing out that networking tends to be evolutionary rather than revolutionary. Before the PC and the PC network a company wanting to computerise had to buy a large mainframe and employ a team of systems analysts and programmers to create a program that would automate the functioning of the whole company. Clearly this endeavour either succeeded or it failed, in which case the expense of the computer and the program was a complete waste. With a PC network things are not so clear cut. If you are already using PCs then they have proved their worth in helping with the existing manual tasks that make the company work. Adding a network cannot reduce the efficiency of the existing PCs and it is very likely to increase their usefulness. If you then go on to add a shared database between sales and dispatch this will automate part of the total operation with the remainder working by established manual methods. By a process of development it should be possible to extend the database so that it replaces all of the existing manual methods and integrates and automates the entire functioning of the company. Of course as the company changes and grows new functions will have to be added to the network but this shouldn't be as big an upheaval as switching from one mainframe to a larger model because you have outgrown it. A network can evolve with your company.

# ALTERNATIVES TO NETWORKING

There are alternatives to networking PCs that are claimed to bring many of the same advantages. In particular an alternative method of sharing data and other resources is the multi-user computer. In this system a single computer is shared by a number of users each with a simple VDU. This is of course the traditional way that computers have been used in the past. It does indeed allow a number of users access to the same data and to share the same printer via printer spooling but it doesn't really fit into a modern view of computing. As well as sharing all of the computing resources that you want to share, a multi-user computer also shares the computer itself and this is usually an unwelcome side effect.

Before the advent of personal computing multi-user operation was necessary because the cost of a computer was so high that it was an economic necessity to share the machine, and hence the cost, among a number of users. The disadvantage was of course that each user only received a fraction of the computing power of the machine. In most users' experience the power of a single dedicated machine is generally insufficient and so the idea of sharing this scarce resource is not a pleasant one. This should be contrasted with the situation in a network where each user has the full attention of a PC. Adding users to a multi-user system always results in a degradation in performance whereas in a network this is a much smaller effect.

This is not to say that multi-user systems cannot work well for some applications. If your application is such that the actual demands made on the computer are small and the tasks do not require any special hardware, such as graphics, then multi-user operation is a possibility. Even then there are two additional considerations that are in favour of a networking option.

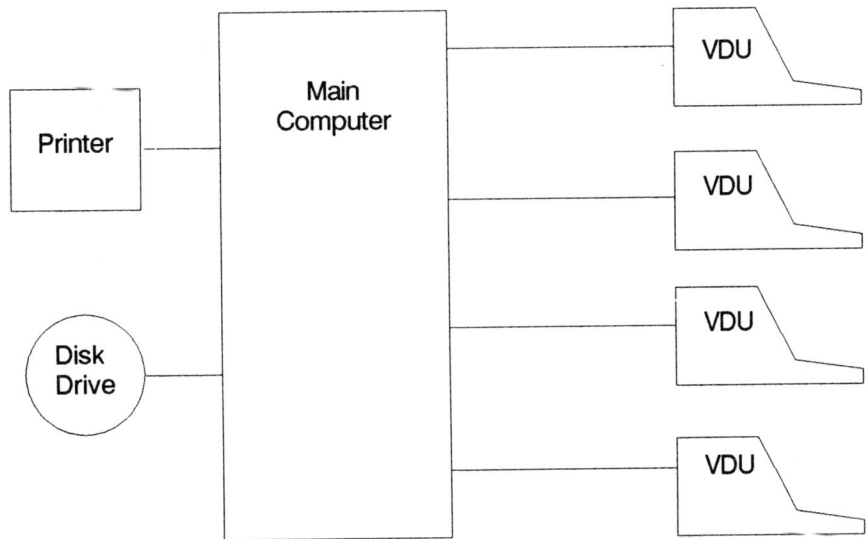

Multi-user computer system

☐   A multi-user set-up concentrates all of the computing power in one machine. This makes a breakdown in any part of the machine affect all users. In a network it is possible to incorporate redundancy so that if one part of the network fails then another PC can take over the functioning of the failed machine. Even if redundancy isn't explicitly designed into a network the worst possible failure still leaves the individual machines capable of functioning as stand alone units.

☐   A multi-user machine has to be bought in one go. This means that you cannot adopt the approach of buying individual PCs and then connecting them together using a network at a later date.

In addition to multi-user there is also a specific alternative to using a network to share a printer. There are specially built pieces of electronics called **printer sharers**. These allow more than one PC to connect to the same printer. The first PC to send output to the printer is allowed to gain control of the printer and until the print job is finished other users are blocked. This is clearly an electronic equivalent of direct connection via a network. If you are only installing a network as a way of sharing a printer then this approach is worth considering as an alternative but you need to be aware that you will have to lay a printer cable from each PC to the printer sharer.

# SUMMARY

■ A network is a way of sharing peripherals and data and of providing E-mail communication.

■ Unlike isolated PCs a network can be involved with the total functioning of a company.

■ The main peripherals that are worth sharing are hard disks and printers.

■ A shared hard disk should be used to provide each PC with access to the applications programs that are needed.

■ The only data files that should be stored on a shared hard disk are those that you need to share.

■ Private data files should be stored on local floppy disk drives.

■ Shared printers should be connected to machines with hard disks.

■ E-mail is a valuable supplement to normal office communications not a replacement for them.

# 2. Hardware for Low Cost PC Networking

In this chapter we take a look at the different types of hardware that can be used to implement a PC network. Although there are many different products on the market they share a surprising number of similarities and it is possible to consider general issues without becoming too bogged down with comparing the merits of one particular system with another. In many ways the hardware can be viewed as the foundation of the network. It makes communications between machines possible but without good network software, **netware**, to go with it even the best communications facilities will be wasted. This means that when buying a real product you have to take into account not only the hardware facilities it offers but the software that either comes with it or can be bought for it.

## HOW FAR? HOW FAST? HOW MANY?

Although manufacturers advertising would have us believe that the most important characteristics of any network are hardware-related, this is something of an overstatement. In principle the only things that the network hardware determines are:

☐ How large a distance can there be between two machines on the network

☐ How fast can data be transferred between machines

☐ How many PCs can be connected together on a single network

In other words, the network hardware mainly determines 'How far, how fast and how many?' There are a number of other factors such as the type and pattern of wiring between machines and compatibility issues that might be important in some situations.

## MEASURING SPEED

There is something of a problem in measuring the speed at which a network can transfer data because theoretical speeds don't necessarily translate into anything realisable. The basic measure of how fast a network operates is the number of bits per second (bps) it can transfer between two or more machines. For example, many networks operate at 1 Mbps or 1 Million bits per second. To get some idea of how fast this is all you need to know is that it takes eight bits to represent a single character. So 1Mbps transfers data at around 125 thousand characters a second. In other words, it should be possible to transfer a 125K file in one second. Of course these estimates ignore the need for control information, such as who the file is for, who it is from, etc., to be transmitted over the network. Another problem is that in many networks the same transmission channel is shared by all the PCs and can drastically reduce the amount of useful data that can be transferred on a network that is reaching its capacity. That is, it is not just the raw transmission speed of the network that determines its capacity to transfer information but how this is actually used.

## NET HARDWARE

There are only a small number of basic variations on how a number of PCs can communicate with each other. However each of these

## Bus network connection

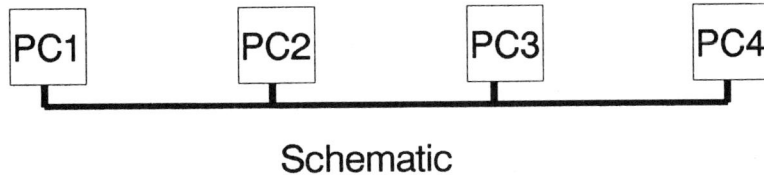

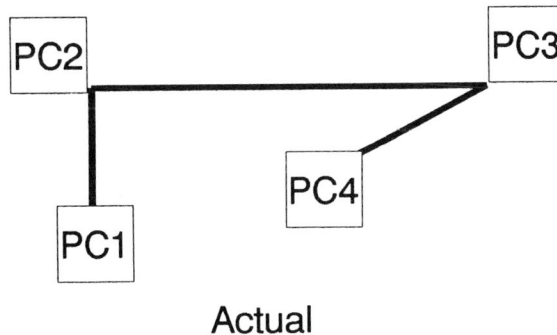

PC1      PC2      PC3      PC4

Schematic

PC2                          PC3

PC4

PC1

Actual

basic variations is capable of almost infinite minor variation as each manufacturer creates their own particular product. In this section enough of the basic concepts of networking hardware are described for you to have a practical appreciation of the different types. If you are interested in the rather more technical internal workings of the basic network types then see Appendix A.

The most common type of PC network uses a single cable to connect all the machines together. This cable threads its way through an office or building, visiting each PC once and then carrying on its way. This arrangement is known as a **bus** configuration and although we will consider cabling issues later in this chapter it is worth examining how a single cable can be used by a number of machines. There are other types of network configuration but the bus is the most often used in low cost networks and it has significant advantages in an office environment.

# THE LISTEN BEFORE SPEAK PRINCIPLE

Humans solved the problem of sharing a single channel of communication long before computers or networks were thought of. If you are in discussion with a group of people then, as long as the discussion is orderly, each potential speaker will wait until the current speaker has finished before starting to talk. The basic principle is that each participant listens and waits for silence before starting to speak. In this way the single shared channel of communication can be used by all of the participants. In a networking context the listen before speak principle is called **Carrier Sense Multiple Access** or **CSMA**. Each PC connected to the bus checks to see that no other PC is transmitting data before sending any data.

If you have followed this description then you might have noticed that there is the possibility that two or more people engaged in the group conversation might listen for silence and accidentally detect it at the same time and so begin speaking at the same time. In network jargon this is called a **collision**. In the case of the human discussion group what happens, or should happen, to handle the collision is that the simultaneous speakers immediately notice that more than one person is talking and they all stop. In network jargon this is called **collision detection**. At this point if each speaker merely applied the same listen before speak principle then they would all start speaking at the same time again and again. In practice there are a number of possible ways that a collision can be resolved. There could be some kind of arbitration between the collided parties or an agreed priority for restarting speaking. In the case of a network the most common collision resolution system is for each PC to hold off or back off from restarting sending their message for a random period of time. In this way one of the PCs will gain access to the bus without competition and the rest will wait until the message has finished. This is usually called **Collision Detection and Collision Avoidance** or **CD/CA**.

There is no real need for you to understand how a single cable is shared by a number of PCs but it does help to see why the maximum data transfer rate of a network may never be achieved. If a network consists of just two PCs or if just two PCs on a larger network are doing all the communicating, then you can achieve the maximum data transfer rate. However, if more than two PCs are involved then there will inevitably be collisions and this reduces the effective transfer rate.

# BUS NETWORKS

It is convenient to divide the common networks into three different types:

☐ Ethernet and Ethernet-like

☐ High speed synchronous

☐ High speed asynchronous

**Ethernet** was one of the first commercial networks and it is backed up by a rigorous standard. However it is a very high performance network and so not really suitable in its complete form for a low cost network. Many manufacturers have followed the general outline of the Ethernet standard but downgraded it in some way, for example by reducing its transmission speed, to reduce its cost. These networks are not Ethernet-compatible but they are very like Ethernet in their general properties.

**High speed synchronous** networks tend to be the product of individual manufacturer's designs and not subject to any standards. The main difference between these networks and the Ethernet types is that they use multi-core cable to distribute not only data signals but system clocks that allow the data to be easily recovered. This represents a significant simplification over the sort of hardware needed to implement Ethernet and so there is a corresponding price reduction. The disadvantage is that usually fewer workstations can be connected and the transmission rates are lower.

**High speed asynchronous** networks are based on the use of the PC's existing serial or RS232 port. In principle the RS232 port that nearly every PC has as standard these days has everything you need to implement a network. It can both receive and transmit data and it has just enough control signals incorporated to be able to sense when the network is silent, and so clear to transmit, and when a transmission error has occurred. High speed asynchronous networks tend to be the lowest cost networks of all but they are usually limited in speed, distance and number of workstations.

# NETWORK ADAPTERS

Although it is possible to create a network using the existing communications ports within a PC, it is more common to add extra hardware in the form of a **network adapter** card. A specially designed network card will usually offer a much higher performance than using the built-in communications port but it also costs more. Ethernet, Ethernet-like and high speed synchronous networks all involve the use of a network adapter. Sometimes the network adapter comes bundled with network software but it is often possible to buy netware from alternative suppliers that will work with the adapter.

Fitting a network adapter is usually very easy. In most cases the card will come set up ready to work in a standard IBM PC/XT. As long as you have a standard machine with no unusual expansion cards already installed then this configuration should work first time. Even so you may have to set a number of DIP switches or jumpers to determine the station number or address that the PC that you are installing will respond to. In most cases each PC connected to the network has to be assigned a unique station number but there are exceptions to this.

If the PC that the network adapter is being installed in is in any way out of the ordinary then the chances are that you will have to alter its configuration. This can involve determining suitable settings for any of:

☐   Base address – the position in the PC's I/O memory map that the network adapter can be found

☐   Interrupt level – the signal that the network adapter uses to signal that it needs attention from the PC

☐   DMA channel – the data channel that the network adapter uses to transfer data to and from the PC's memory

Not all network adapters use all of these facilities and in some cases they are simply set to fixed values. In practice the problem is to find settings that do not conflict with existing expansion cards. This is usually possible but in an extreme case it may be necessary to modify the settings of existing expansion cards. The effect of clashes between the network adapter and another card in the PC obviously depends on the type of card that the clash occurs with. In general a clash usually manifests itself as either a system crash after using the resources of the card in question or the failure of the card to provide the facility. It is not likely that any actual damage will be done to either of the cards involved in the clash but the problem has to be resolved to ensure the smooth running of a network. For example, in the case of one network it proved impossible to use a modem card without crashing the PC in which it was installed. No harm was caused to the functioning of the rest of the network, it was simply inconvenient to have to restart the machine each time a comms package was used. The problem was caused by the network card and the modem both using interrupt level 2. The solution was to simply change the network adapter to use interrupt level 3.

Determining which base address, interrupt level and DMA channel to use is a very technical business. Appendix B gives details of the usual assignments found in PCs and ATs to help you find a free setting. Technical though it might be, it has to be admitted that in practice configuring a network adapter can often be a matter of trial and error. The best approach is to try the manufacturer's default setting until a problem arises. Then attempt to identify the card with which the clash is occurring and try to discover its settings and alter one of the two cards to avoid the conflict.

If the discussion of configuring a network adapter sounds fraught with difficulty, it is worth repeating that in most cases there is no need to alter the manufacturer's setting – but it pays to be aware of the possibilities.

## CABLING

Surprisingly, for all their sophisticated claims, one of the biggest differences between networks is their cabling requirements. It sounds rather strange to say that from a practical point of view type of cabling is the most important feature of a network but this isn't far from being true. In general the faster the network the more critical and expensive is the cabling. This fact alone can sometimes mean that a lower speed network is preferable.

There are four major types of cable and cabling system:

☐ Ethernet

☐ Cheapernet

☐ Twisted pair

☐ Multi-core or RS232

and these will be described in turn.

# ETHERNET CABLING

The Ethernet cabling system is the only one to be fully defined by a standard. The standard is a very exacting one and as a result the cable and its extras constitute the most expensive way to install a network. The cable itself is very thick, over 1cm coaxial cable, and costs roughly £2.00 per metre. Its thickness means that it can be difficult to thread into existing cable runs and this also adds to its expense. The advantage of Ethernet cable is that it permits a network to operate very fast (10Mbps) and over large distances.

Another feature almost unique to Ethernet is that each workstation is connected to the cable via a special transceiver. The transceiver can be thought of as a tap point in the cable and the PC is connected to it by up to 50 metres of special transceiver cable. This means that, unlike many of the lower cost networking systems, the main Ethernet cable doesn't have to visit each of the machines in turn. Instead it can take a more or less central route through the office or building and as long as each PC is within 50 metres they can be reached by transceiver taps. The transceiver cable is a thinner multi-pair cable but it is rather more expensive than Ethernet cable proper and each transceiver can cost as much as £250.

There are two ways of connecting a transceiver to an Ethernet cable – **N series connectors** or an **intrusive tap**. An N series connector is a coaxial connector (rather like a TV aerial plug) that has a screw fitting cover that joins cable very firmly together. Using N series connectors inserting a transceiver into a cable is a matter of shutting down the system, cutting the cable, putting N series connectors on each of the cut ends and then rejoining the cable using the transceiver. Using an intrusive tap has the advantage that a transceiver can be connected to an existing system without first shutting it down. To do this you have to use a special tool to drill a hole in the Ethernet cable to pierce the outer shielding and reach the inner conductor. The transceiver then has a special connector in

10.3mm

PVC

Outer Braid

Aluminised Tape

Inner Braid

Insulator

Copper conductor

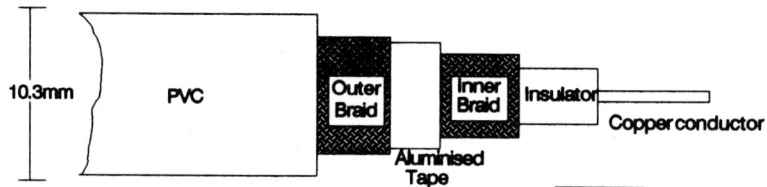

**Ethernet cable**

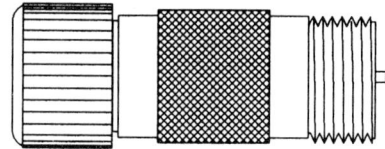

**N series connector**

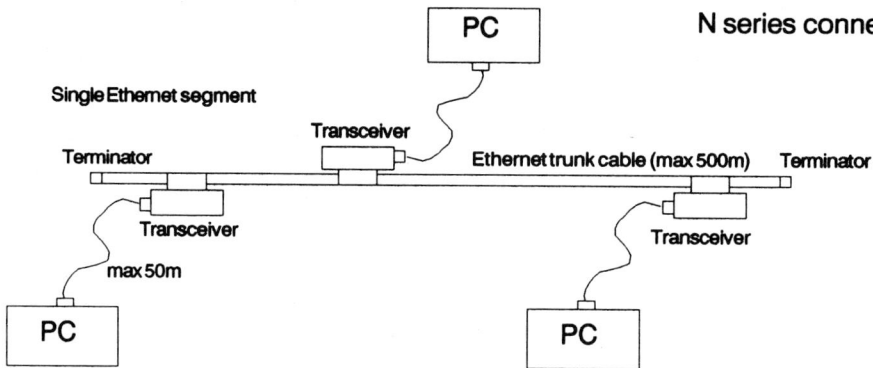

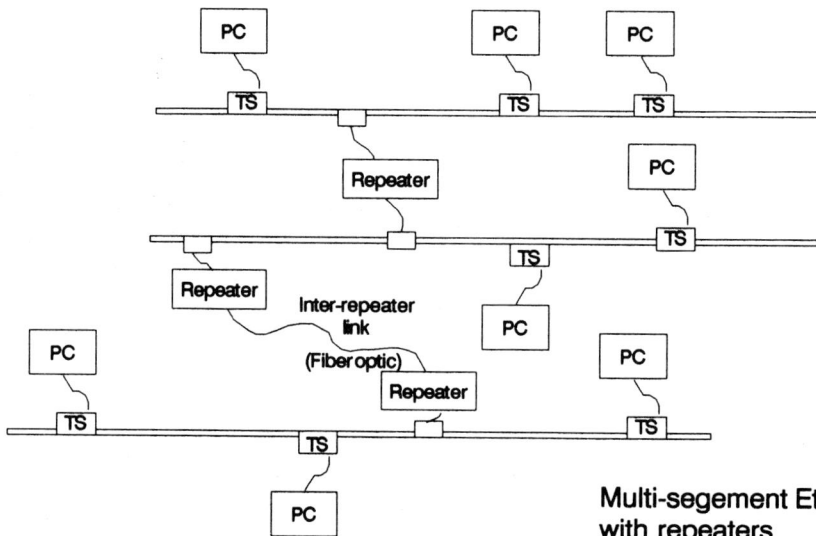

PC

**Single Ethernet segment**

Transceiver

Terminator

Ethernet trunk cable (max 500m)

Terminator

Transceiver

max 50m

Transceiver

PC

PC

PC

PC

PC

TS

TS

TS

Repeater

PC

TS

Repeater

TS

PC

Inter-repeater link

(Fiber optic)

Repeater

PC

PC

TS

TS

TS

PC

**Multi-segement Ethernet with repeaters**

the form of a clamp which, as it is tightened on the cable, inserts a sharp pin through the hole in the cable and then makes contact with the central copper wire.

In principle this operation can be performed while the network is operating but evidence suggests that if possible shutting the network down while a new tap is made is a good precaution. The connection from the transceiver box to the PC is made via a 9-pin D connector. Transceivers can be placed anywhere on the Ethernet cable but there is a restriction that the minimum distance between tap points is 2.5 metres. Also the number of taps on a single piece of Ethernet cable is restricted to 100 and hence this is also the number of workstations that can be supported.

The only other point to note is that the Ethernet cable has to be terminated correctly at each end. This has to be done to ensure that unwanted reflections of the signal from either end of the cable are minimised. This is a common requirement for network cabling and in the case of Ethernet is achieved by using two special N series connectors that contain 50 ohm resistors.

The maximum number of workstations, or equivalently trans-ceivers, that can be connected to one section of Ethernet cable is 100 and the maximum length of a single segment is 500 metres. In some cases you may want to go beyond these limitations, especially the maximum 500 metres length. (However notice that as the Ethernet cable only has to come within 50 metres of each PC you can generally get further with 500 metres of Ethernet cable than other types of network cable that have to follow the outline of an office to reach every PC.)

The solution to the number of workstations and maximum length problem is to join together additional cable segments using a **repeater**. A repeater, as its name suggests, is simply a device that passes the signals on each segment of the cable from one to another.

The use of a repeater as a way of extending the length of a network cable is not unique to Ethernet. In this case the limits are raised to a maximum of five segments totalling 2500 metres. This sounds good but there is also a limit on the distance between two workstations and the number of repeaters that can be between them. Only workstations that are less than 1500 metres apart and separated by a maximum of two repeaters can communicate. You may find that manufacturers vary these limits a little and there are ways to increase them, but for a simple Ethernet installation you should think of 1500 metres of cable as a workable maximum. (There are repeaters that can be used to increase the range to a maximum of 3 kilometres but these are £1500 each and a total of five are necessary!)

As the discussion above suggests, a true Ethernet installation is not cheap. Indeed it barely comes into the category of a low cost LAN! It is doubtful if many PC users would choose to use Ethernet from scratch. Its importance is that it represents a standard that many other networks try to imitate at reduced costs. Even so it is possible that you might have to integrate a planned PC LAN with an existing Ethernet system and in this case you need to know something about Ethernet in its own right. Ethernet is also one of the few networks that can support a range of different machines.

# CHEAPERNET

In an effort to reduce the cabling costs of Ethernet while retaining much of its high speed performance, many manufacturers have introduced Cheapernet as alternative. Cheapernet is almost identical to Ethernet and transmits data at the same speed, 10Mbps. It differs by dispensing with the use of transceivers in favour of a lower cost coaxial cable and direct BNC series connectors. Many Ethernet network adapter cards can drive either true Ethernet cable via a suitable transceiver or a Cheapernet cable directly from electronics on the adapter.

5mm | PVC | Insulator | Wire core | Copper Braid

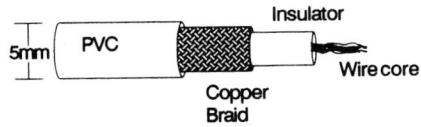

**Cheapernet cable**

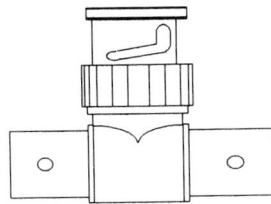

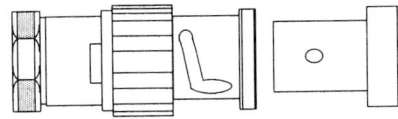

**BNC connector**    **BNC socket**

**BNC T connector**

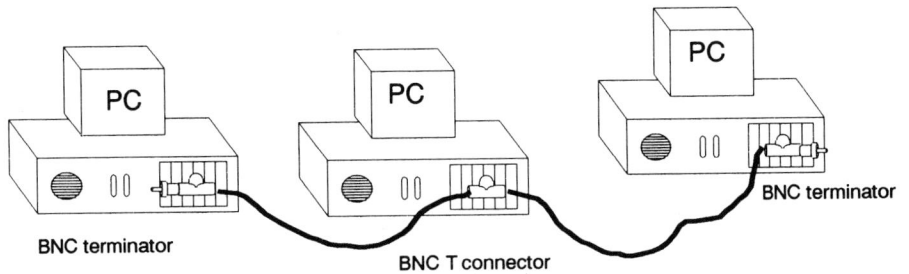

PC    PC    PC

BNC terminator    BNC T connector    BNC terminator

**Cheapernet segment (300m max)**

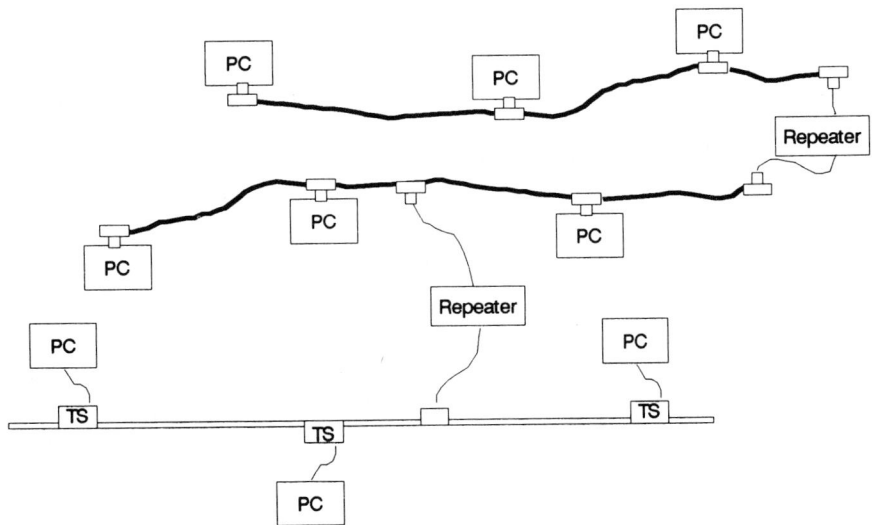

PC    PC    PC

Repeater

PC    PC    PC

Repeater

PC    PC

PC    TS    TS    TS

PC

**Multi-segement Cheapernet mixed with Ethernet**

Simply disposing of the transceiver means that Cheapernet saves £250 per workstation. The cable used is also thinner at 0.5cm and cheaper at around 30p per metre. The thinness of the cable is responsible for the system's other common name **Thin cable Ethernet**. The increased flexibility of the cable means that it can be routed through existing cable ducts more easily than thick Ethernet cable.

The main disadvantage of Cheapernet is that the maximum length of a single segment of cable is reduced to 300 metres. As in the case of Ethernet, segments of cable can be joined using repeaters and in this case the maximum is 3 segments using 2 repeaters over 900 metres. This may sound like a small reduction over Ethernet's 500 metres and 1500 metres but there is another effect to consider. Dispensing with the use of transceivers means that the Cheapernet cable has to be routed to each of the workstations in turn. This means that it has to follow the contours of the office or building visiting each desk or room that has a PC once. Clearly the twists and turns involved in this will use up cable at a faster rate than a simple straight line measurement would suggest.

The connection system used by Cheapernet is based on **BNC series connectors**. These are coaxial connectors (rather like a TV aerial plug) with a push and twist lock fitting. They are more reliable than other types of connector but not as good as the Ethernet N series connectors. The actual connection to each machine is made via a BNC T adapter. The Cheapernet cable comes into the machine on one side of the T and leaves to visit the remaining machines from the other side of the T. The minimum distance between two machines is 3 metres. The only other complication is that each segment of cable has to be terminated using 50 ohm resistors. This is most easily done using special BNC 50 ohm terminating plugs on the last sections of cable. Notice that, unlike Ethernet in which each segment is one piece of cable, a Cheapernet segment is made up of lengths of cable joined together at each machine by BNC T adapters.

As Ethernet and Cheapernet only differ in the type of cables that they use it is possible to join an Ethernet cable section to a Cheapernet cable section. To do this you need a transceiver to tap into the Ethernet cable and a repeater to make the connection between the two systems.

# TWISTED PAIR

Twisted pair is simply a cable consisting of two wires twisted together for the entire length of the cable. The twisting is important because it determines the characteristics of the cable and provides a measure of protection against electrical noise. The actual cable used varies from manufacturer to manufacturer and there is no real standard. However in most cases the cable is as thin and flexible as a phone cable. It is also the lowest cost cable at around 20p per metre. Its disadvantage it that it can only be used reliably at 1Mbps, that is ten times slower than an Ethernet or Cheapernet system. Other specifications of a twisted pair network depend very much on the exact details of the manufacturer's implementation and recommendations for reliable working. However it is possible to state some reasonable working parameters. The maximum length of a twisted pair segment is roughly 300 metres, the same as a Cheapernet system. Each segment can cope with around 32 workstations and at most four 300 metre segments can be connected together using repeaters giving a total workable length of 1200 metres.

Like the Cheapernet cabling system, a twisted pair has to visit each machine in turn. The connections to the network adapter card are usually made via low cost US-style telephone jacks. This has the added advantage that network tap boxes can be fixed to the wall

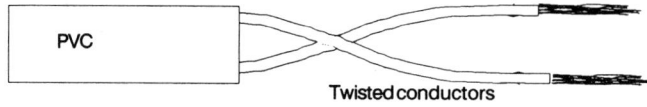

Twisted conductors

Twisted pair cable

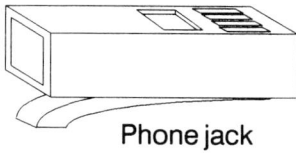

Phone jack

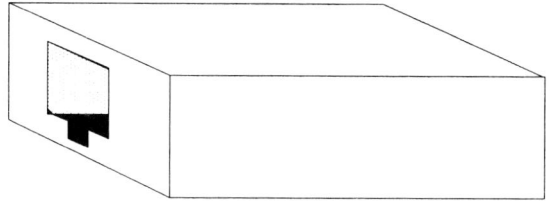

Socket

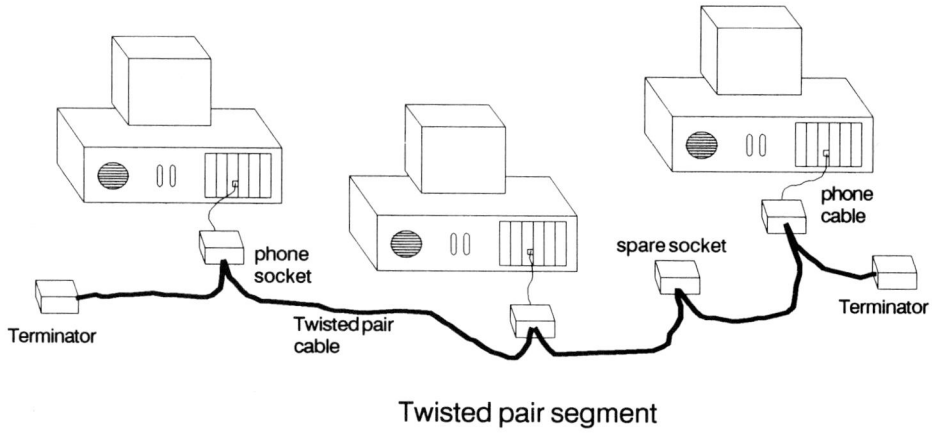

Twisted pair segment

close to the machine that they are intended to serve and phone cable used to complete the connection. This means that machines can be easily added to and removed from the network at any time. The cable usually has to be terminated correctly and this is often accomplished by mounting a 100 ohm resistor in two final tap boxes at each end of the cable run. Alternatively some network cards give the option of enabling a terminating resistor by setting a jumper or DIP switch on the machines at either end of the cable. This has the advantage of simplicity, but it runs the risk of bringing the whole network down if the two end machines are accidentally disconnected.

Twisted pair is simple to install, low cost and its only disadvantage is a reduced transmission rate. However this is still a respectable 1Mbps and this is enough for all but the most demanding networks application. For these reasons it is quickly becoming so popular as to be the standard for low cost PC networks. Its only real danger is that upgrading to faster Ethernet system should 1Mbps prove insufficient would mean starting from scratch.

# MULTI-CORE OR RS232

A multi-core cable is exactly what its name suggests – a single cable containing a number of wires. Instead of using a single signal cable as in the case of Ethernet, Cheapernet and twisted pair, networks that make use of multi-core cable use more than one cable to transmit data and possibly control information or a clock signal. Networks that make use of this system are the most diverse of all. Some simply transmit the data, others transmit data and a timing clock pulse. Transmission rates vary from 1Mbps down to .1Mbps and even lower. Some networks allow you to vary the transmission rate with the length of cable in use, so permitting the user to choose between a slow long network or a fast short network. Typical maximum network lengths are 200 metres.

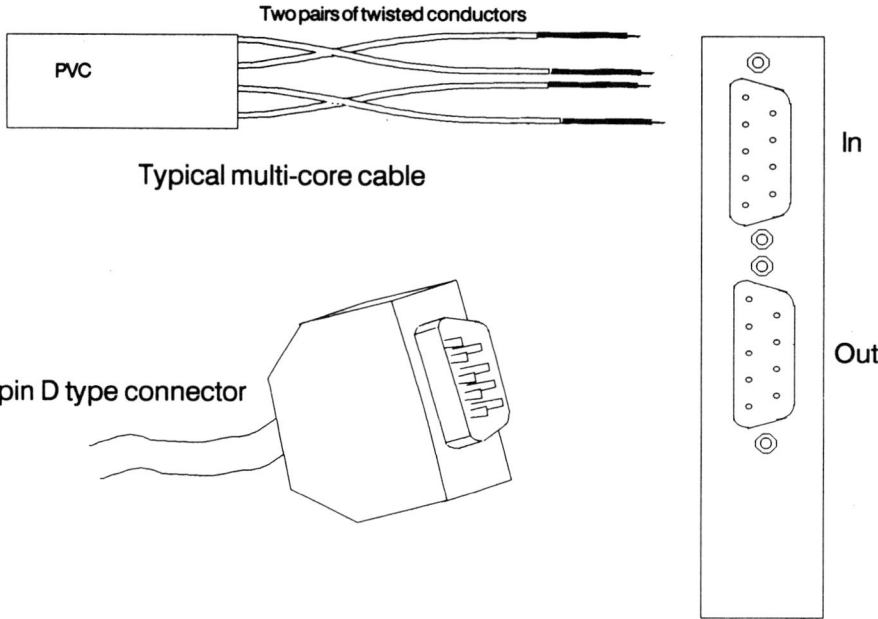

Two pairs of twisted conductors

PVC

Typical multi-core cable

In

9-pin D type connector

Out

Single segment multi-core

Although there is no standard for connectors many networks use a 9-pin D connector. Usually the wiring has to go from machine to machine and the network adapters often have a male and a female 9-pin D connector, one for the incoming cable and one for the outgoing cable. The machines at each end of the cable usually have to have a special termination plug fitted to the unused sockets.

Even though the 9-pin D connector is very common, many networks that use multi-core cable use their own method of connection. For example, networks that use the PC's standard serial port incorporate a standard phone connector. In general this group of networks is more suited to small office and ad-hoc installations.

## OTHER TYPES OF NETWORK

There are many types of network other than those described above but most of them do not fall into the category of low cost LANs. In particular you are bound to come across the networks that use both the token ring and the star configuration approach.

A **token ring** is different from a bus network in that the network cable visits each computer in turn but also connects the first machine to the last to form a ring. In some situations this wiring pattern is very suitable but in others it can be a nuisance to have return the cable from the last computer that you connect to the first. However the actual connection pattern of the network isn't always clearly reflected in the cabling pattern. For example, the best known ring is the IBM Token ring and this is cabled as a star (see later) by bringing all the cables together in a central connector box which then joins them together in a ring!

In practice most token rings are configured as groups of small rings connected together by communications bridges. The advantage of a

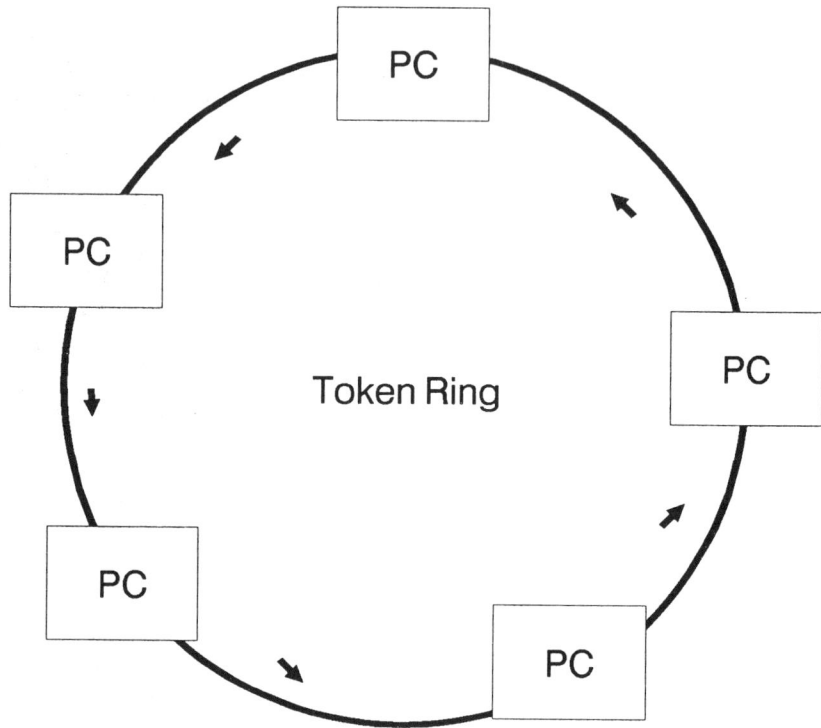

token ring is that it uses a different method of allowing each machine to use the network cable. Essentially what happens is that a particular pattern of data – a **token** is transmitted round the ring. Each machine that receives the token passes it on to the next machine in the ring unless it wants to transmit a message. The only time that a machine can transmit a message is when it has received the token and so this controls access to the network. For more information see Appendix A. It is the use of a token to control access to the network that is the real difference between the ring and the bus type of network. Indeed it is possible to implement a token access system on a bus network simply by defining an order that the machines take turns in transmitting data.

Token rings are ideal for situations where each machine needs a guaranteed portion of time to transmit data. This gives token rings a significant advantage over bus networks in factory automation, robots, process control, etc. In an office environment they have very little to recommend them unless the network is intended to grow to include hundreds of workstations.

In a **star network** each machine is connected to a central 'hub' or controller. The hub acts as a message switching centre and so enables each machine to communicate with every other machine. The disadvantage of a star network is that the operation of the whole network depends on the correct functioning of the hub. Develop a hardware problem in the hub and the whole network stops. Also the siting of the hub in a convenient position can be difficult. It can be very irritating to have to use hundreds of metres of cable to connect two machines that are on adjacent desks. However star networks can deal with large numbers of work-stations over very large distances typically 6000 metres. Star networks are currently very expensive when compared to alternative PC networks.

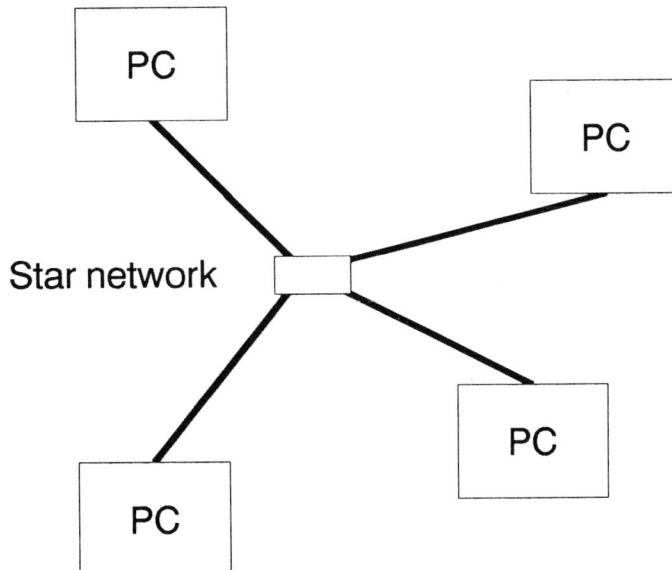

Star network

PC

PC

PC

PC

# REFLECTIONS

One of the biggest problems with most networks is that they usually have very precise specifications that the manuals suggest cannot be varied. For example, the type of cable, connector and the maximum length of cable are usually exactly defined. When you come to install a network the situation nearly always arises that a slight change in the wiring standards would make things simpler or better. Usually if you ask the manufacturer if a change is in order the answer will be no. The reason for this is that most of the technical people employed by network companies are software experts and it is safer to stick to the rules.

In practice it is usually possible to break the wiring rules and still run a reliable network. However if you do go outside of the specification and a problem arises then don't be surprised if the network company blames the change in wiring! The remainder of this section is fairly technical and if you have no intention of modifying the wiring layout specified for a network then it can be safely skipped.

Network cabling is more critical than say mains cabling or telephone cabling because it carries signals that have frequency components all the way up to 10Mhz and in some cases higher. To give you some idea how high a frequency this is it is worth saying that FM radio uses 100Mhz. In other words, network cabling is more like cable TV than anything else! Most of the problems described below really only affect the higher speed systems such as Ethernet and Cheapernet.

The most important characteristic of such cable transmission systems is the **cable impedance**. Roughly speaking this can be thought of as the resistance of the cable to the signal that is passing along it. As long as a cable has a constant impedance there are no problems. If however there is a sudden change in the cable's impedance then a proportion of the signal is reflected back down the cable. This is a phenomenon very similar to the effect different transparent materials have on light. Each time a beam of light strikes a material of a different optical density, glass from air say, a portion of the beam is transmitted and a portion reflected. In normal use a signal cable does have a constant impedance and so there are no troublesome reflections to interfere with the signal. However there are two places in every cable where the impedance changes unless steps are taken to make sure that it doesn't – the two ends of the cable!

At a free end the cable's impedance becomes infinite and so there is a total reflection of the signal. To avoid the problem the cable has to be terminated using a resistor of the same impedance as the cable. This is the reason for the need to correctly terminate all of the cabling systems described above. If a terminator fails for some reason then the network is likely to become unreliable, or even stop working altogether, due to reflections from the end of the cable.

As well as reflections from the end of the cable, any discontinuity has the potential to set up reflections. In particular, each connector has to be made to present the same impedance as the cable and each T adapter in a Cheapernet system has to split the signal without changing the impedance. As long as you do not introduce large impedance changes in the cable then variations in the wiring layout should be possible. For example, you can join two pieces of cable together as long as you use the correct type of plug and socket. Just joining the cable using a terminal block or by soldering isn't good enough because of the change in impedance that this would introduce. In the same way you must always use a BNC T adapter to split a Cheapernet cable. If you simply wire the cable into a tee the result would be unacceptable because of the reflections set up by the change in impedance.

A second problem with high speed cables is that of standing waves. This can happen if a section of cable happens to be exactly the right length to **resonate** to the signal that it is carrying. In principle this resonating only happens because of reflections caused by impedance changes, but if a section of cable happens to be the right length a small reflection can build up into a major problem. This is the reason that the Ethernet specification says that two transceivers have to be more than 2.5 metres apart. For the same reason each section of Cheapernet cable should be longer than 3 metres.

# PHYSICAL DETAILS OF CABLING

Although it is usually better to get an expert in to do the cabling for a permanent installation, you may want to install your own test network for a few machines. In general this is entirely possible and you can simply leave the cable draped around the office until it is properly installed. However it is important that you run the cable so that it avoids mains cables and fluorescent lights and any other source of electrical noise in the office.

It is also important that the cable is protected from mechanical damage. Pressure on the cable can deform it and change its electrical characteristics, even if the damage isn't so bad as to actually sever the connection. You can buy plastic cable bridges to protect the cable if it has to cross part of the office where people walk. It is not good enough to simply push the cable under the carpet and try to forget about it! You can also use double sided tape to secure network sockets and other wall mounting units until the network is installed permanently. There are also self-adhesive cable clips that can be used to secure network cable around the office. But be warned – these generally stick so well that when you try to remove them the plaster comes off!

If electrical noise is a problem and you are installing a twisted pair network you can use a shielded twisted pair cable but this severely reduces the working distance. Typically using a shielded twisted pair cable halves the working distance. You can mix shielded and unshielded cable in the same network to maximise the working distance while reducing noise problems.

If you do decide to go in for DIY cabling you should also be aware of building regulations. In particular cables running through a building can be a fire hazard by providing a route along which fire can spread from office to office. To stop this cable can be encased in a conduit. An alternative is to use Plenum cable. This is treated with Teflon and can withstand extreme heat without giving off noxious gases. Plenum cable is so-called because many building regulations insist on its use for cabling in the air space, or plenum, between a suspended ceiling and the actual ceiling.

# SUMMARY

■ Bus network systems, where all the PCs share the same cable for transmitting and receiving data, are the most common low cost LAN systems.

■ The 'listen before speak' principle is used to share the single network cable.

■ The speed of a network is measured in bits per second or bps.

■ The actual rate of useful data transfer on a network depends on far too many factors to enable the raw transmission speed to be used to compare networks but it does set a theoretical upper limit on performance.

■ Bus networks tend to use four types of cabling system:
   Ethernet       – expensive but high performance
   Cheapernet     – as Ethernet but more limited range and cheaper
   Twisted pair   – slower than Ethernet/Cheapernet but often the best price/performance for many office systems
   Multi-core     – lowest cost systems. Very suitable for small or ad hoc office systems.

■ The ring and star are two common alternative patterns of network connection.

■ The cabling used by a network does not always follow the pattern of actual connections.

■ The token ring is a high performance network suitable for factory automation or very large office networks

■ Care has to be taken when joining cable not to alter its electrical characteristics.

■ Cable should be routed to avoid electrical noise and should be protected from mechanical stress.

# 3. Software for Low Cost PC Networking

In this chapter we examine the important role that software plays in a successful network. Although the hardware components of any network tend to dominate in the early stages of choosing a network it is important to realise that the software is responsible for delivering the potential of the network to the user. In short the network hardware determines the maximum rate at which information can be transferred across the network and the wiring pattern but the rest is the responsibility of the software.

Although there is much diversity in network software all **network operating systems** have to tackle the same range of problems and deliver similar facilities. They tend to differ in the exact ways that they solve these problems, how they implement the facilities and in which facilities they choose to ignore, but they are all concerned with sharing network resources and allowing users to communicate.

In the early days of networking so much of the effort went into constructing the hardware necessary to implement the network that there was very little left over to work on the software. It was a huge undertaking to build Ethernet or similar hardware and there was almost an attitude that the software to use the network was someone else's problem. Now network cards are cheap and most of their functions can be bought off-the-shelf as standard integrated circuits. This means that a larger proportion of the effort to produce a marketable network can now go into software development and as a result there are now a number of excellent network operating systems for the PC.

# SERVERS AND REQUESTERS

Each PC on the network can be classified according to its role. Some machines will allow other machines to share their resources such as disk drives and printers. These machines serve the requests of other machines on the network and so they are called **network servers**. A machine that has no server functions and only makes requests of other machines is called a **requester** or a **client**. It is also possible for a machine to offer services to the network and to make use of services offered by other machines, that is to be a **server/requester**.

Some networks demand that servers are dedicated to the role of serving the network and cannot also be used as standard workstations. Such a **dedicated server** can increase the speed of response to the workstations in the rest of the network and it can get round some of the problems in using MS-DOS as a network operating system (see later) but in general it is too expensive an option for a low cost network and indeed is usually unnecessary. A **non-dedicated server** is simply a workstation that can be used like any other while it simultaneously responds to requests from other workstations.

The advantage of this approach is obviously the saving of the cost of an additional workstation and the disadvantage is that the user of the non-dedicated server will occasionally be slowed down by requests from other users. The effect of such slowing down will depend to a great extent on what the user is trying to do. So the decision about which user is allocated to a non-dedicated server can

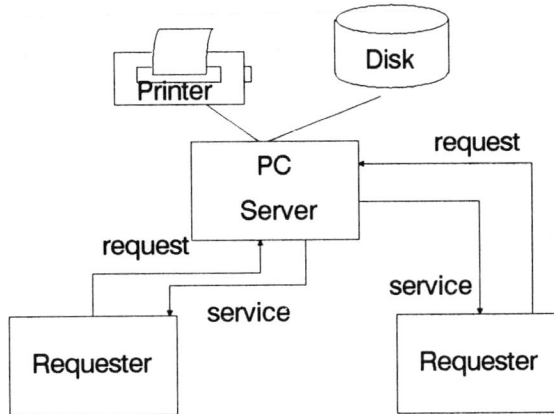

Server/requesters

make a lot of difference to overall user satisfaction with the network. The best guide is to try to allocate a task that is very undemanding of resources to such a PC. Ideally this should be a data input task which does not involve a lot of computation or frequent disk use but the temperament and personality of the user can be equally important factors.

# POWER

Another factor to consider in the design of a network is the type of machine to be used for each workstation. There are now a range of PC type machines which vary in power according to the micro-processor that they use. The original PC/XT and its associated clones use the 8088 or 8086 processor. These are the slowest machines and ideally they should be allocated to the role of requesters. The PC/AT uses the 80286 processor which is roughly twice as fast as an equivalent 8086 type machine. Many network designers recommend the use of a 286 for all servers. Finally there is a new range of machines based on the 80386 which provide maximum performance and more than enough power for most server applications.

Although there is an obvious advantage in using the most powerful machines in the role of network servers it is worth saying that many networks function perfectly well using standard PCs. It all depends on the level of demand placed on the servers and hence the type of use that the network is put to. In addition many networks are constructed using a set of existing PCs with few or no additions. If it is feasible to buy one or two new machines then it is usually worth investing in at least PC/ATs or 386 machines to use as network servers.

# NETWORK TYPES

There are three different types of network organisation depending on the allocation of servers and requesters:

☐ homogeneous

☐ single server

☐ mixed

It is important to realise that almost any network hardware or software can be used to realise a network of one of the above three types. The type of network that you eventually design is mainly a function of the role of the network in your organisation.

In a **homogeneous** network every machine is both a server and a requester. This means that every machine can share the resources of every other machine. In many ways this is the most complicated arrangement for users to cope with. It takes a lot of organisation to make the relationships between the different workstations clear to the users. Either that or each user has to have sufficient knowledge of computing, and specifically of the way the network functions, to be able to make use of its facilities as the need arises. In general homogeneous networks are small, usually no more than three or four machines working on a single or very similar task.

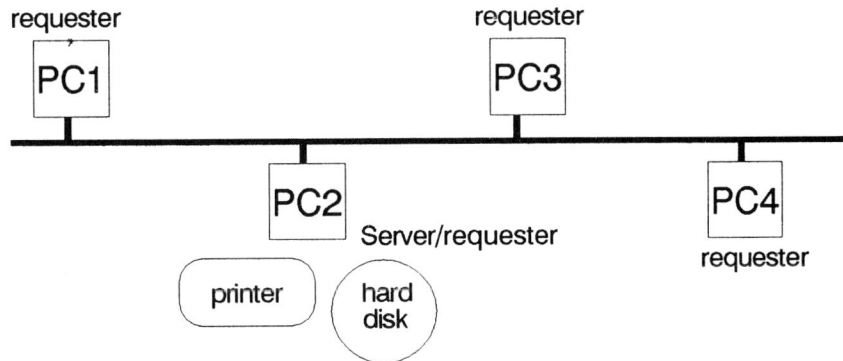

requester

**PC1**

requester

**PC3**

**PC2**

Server/requester

printer    hard disk

**PC4**

requester

## Single server network

In a **single server** or **central server** network all the machines bar one are requesters and a single machine provides all of the network services. This is the simplest type of network from the users' point of view and by far the most common. The single or central server can be dedicated or used as one of the workstations. Each workstation uses the single server for all network resources and so the network tends to look the same from each workstation and so to each user. In general single server networks are suited to the sharing of applications programs and high cost printers.

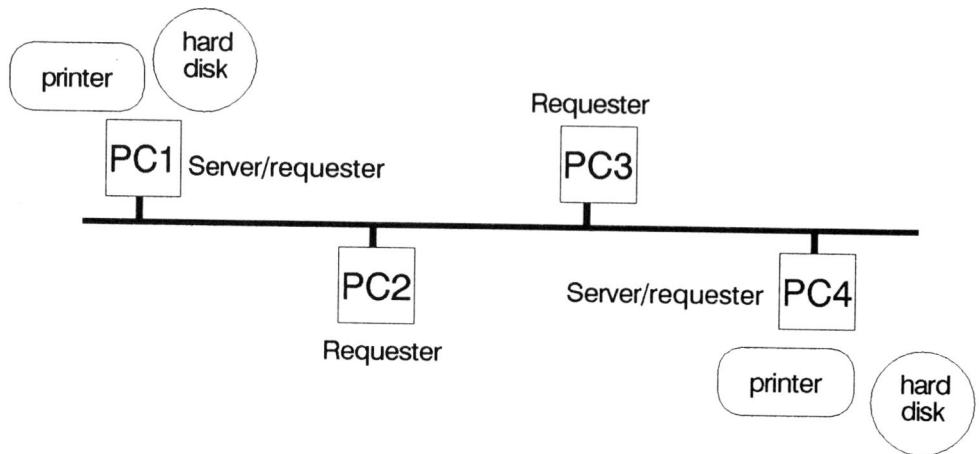

## Mixed network

The **mixed network** is similar to a single server network but with more than one server. There are two distinct types of mixed network depending on whether each requester always uses the same server or not. If each requester does always use the same server then the situation is more like a number of single server networks that just happen to be connected together. For example, if all of the machines in accounts use one server and all the machines in sales use another server then apart from the ability for machines in accounts to communicate with machines in sales the system looks like two single server networks.

A more complicated situation is where some machines use two or more servers either at the same or different times. As long as the network is well organised so that the different servers supply facilities connected with distinct activities it should look simple enough to the users. For example, if one machine supplies word-processing facilities and another database then it is a natural for the

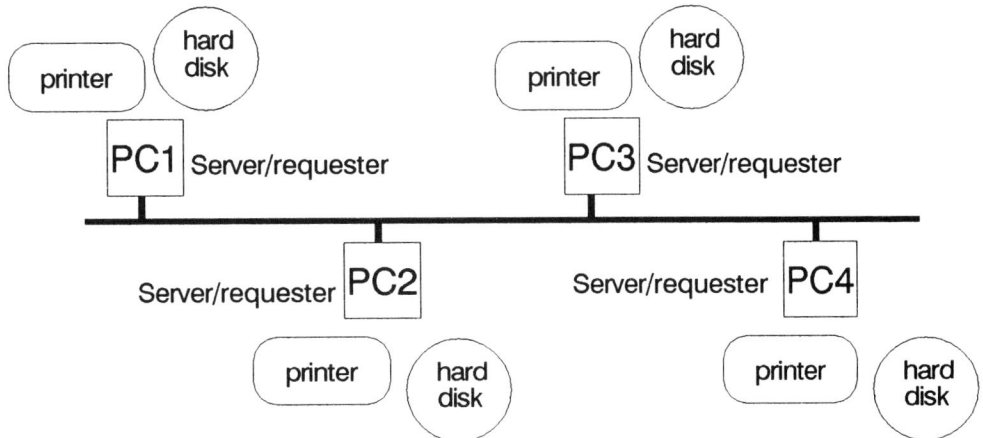

## Homogeneous network

user to switch server as it is to change diskettes. Another common situation is for a user to choose which server to use according to the type of printer being offered.

One important reason for implementing a mixed network is the question of **redundancy**. If a whole network depends on the correct functioning of a single server then a fault in this one machine can mean the disruption of the entire network. A more fault tolerant network can be implemented if at least two servers more or less identical in their specification are available. Normal working would mean that just one of the two possible servers was used – so producing a single server network. If a fault occurred in the main server then it would or should be a simple matter to transfer its responsibilities to the second server.

Many mixed networks start with this well-intentioned simple plan but often become more complicated because knowledgeable users discover that the second server is present in the system and start making use of it! Designing true redundancy into a network is very important if you want it to be fault tolerant.

# *LOG ON AND OFF*

When a machine is first switched on it is generally not part of the network even if it is physically attached. To take part in the running of the network a machine usually has to be connected in the software sense by the user logging on. If a machine is logged off the network then it can be used as a standard isolated PC. Once it is logged on it can take part in the network activity. There is an obvious difference between servers and requesters as regards logging on and off the network. Requesters can log on and off at will without affecting anyone else, but every station that serves the network has to be logged on for the entire time that the network could be required and must not log off without checking whether anyone is using the service it provides.

It is often a good idea for a server to know that a requester has actually logged off the network. For example, if a workstation fails or its power is switched off while using a server how does the server know that it should close open files and generally tidy up after the workstation that has gone? Some networks make no provision for this sort of situation and this can cause other users problems. However most networks cause each workstation to send a **heart beat** signal every so often to indicate that they are still functioning. If a server notices that the heart beat is missing for a period of time then it assumes that the workstation has logged off or gone off and hopefully deals with the event without any fuss.

# REQUESTER FUNCTIONS

Ideally an applications program should be able to run in a requester workstation without being aware of the fact that some of its requests to use devices are being met by a server. This means that the application program should be able to access all devices via MS-DOS in exactly the same way and irrespective of the fact that devices may belong to the workstation that is **local** or have to be accessed over the network that is **remote**. The most usual way of achieving this is to use an additional piece of software called a **redirector**. The role of the redirector is to intercept calls that the applications program makes to MS-DOS and decide if they can be met locally or have to be passed over the network, i.e. redirected to the server concerned. Microsoft introduced a redirector module for use in IBM's own PC Network. Other network implementors have either licensed the Microsoft redirector or produced their own version of it.

At the same time that Microsoft introduced their redirector they also added important networking facilities to MS-DOS Version 3. So important are these networking facilities that you can almost divide all networking software into those that make use of or are compatible with MS-DOS Version 3 and those that are not. The facilities that MS-DOS Version 3 introduced will be discussed later.

No matter what sort of network software you are using, there has to be some method of setting up the connection between a requester and a server. The most usual way of presenting this to a user is to provide a list of local devices and remote devices along with the names by which they are known at the workstation. For example, a workstation may have a single local floppy disk drive called A: and be connected to a remote hard disk drive on a server which is known as drive C:. This is simple as long as each user always uses the same workstation. If this is not the case things can be confusing

```
┌─────────────────────────────────────────────┐
│ Applications program                         │
│ Wordprocessor/spreadsheet/Database           │
└─────────────────────────────────────────────┘
                       ↕
     Requests to use disk drives/printers etc.
                       ↕
┌─────────────────────────────────────────────┐
│                                              │
│                  MSDOS                        │
│                                              │
└─────────────────────────────────────────────┘
                       ↕
        ┌─────────────────────────────┐
        │          Redirector          │
        └─────────────────────────────┘
         ↕            ↕            ↕
   ┌─────────┐  ┌─────────┐
   │         │  │         │   C: = disk D:
   │ Local   │  │ Local   │       on station 004
   │ drive A:│  │ drive B:│
   │         │  │         │
   └─────────┘  └─────────┘
                       ↕
                ┌─────────────┐
                │  Network     │         Data transfer
                │  hardware    │  ←───→     over the
                │     &        │           network
                │  software    │
                └─────────────┘
```

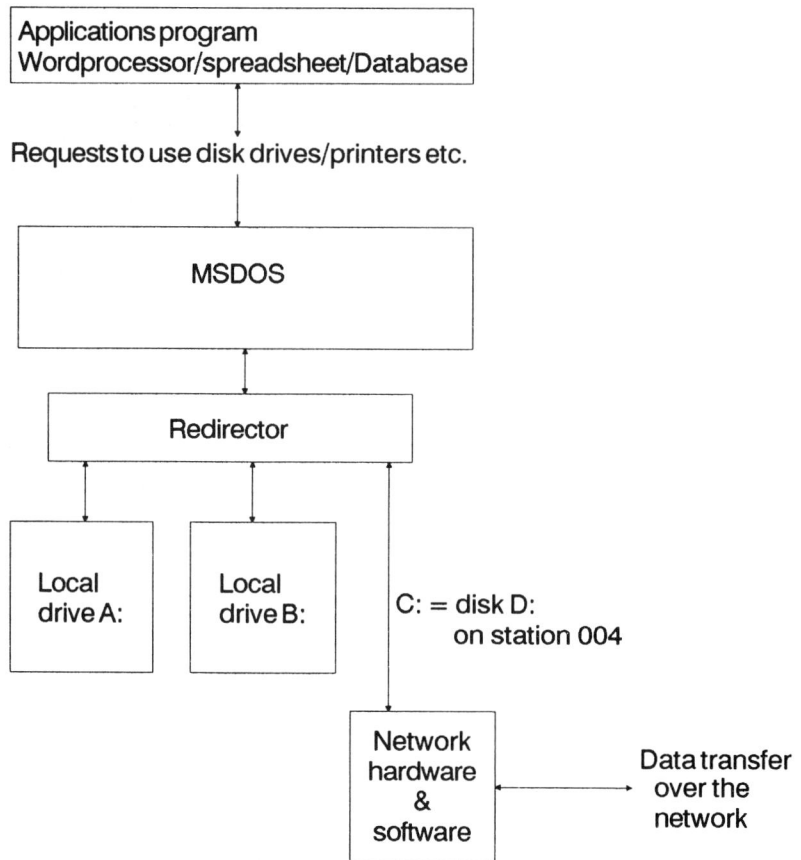

## Requester functions

because one station's drive C: could be another station's drive D: and so on.. !

The allocation of drive letters to local and remote drives is often shown by network software in the form of a table showing who owns the drive and even what the access rights are, etc. The same idea can be used to handle remote printers and even communications ports. For example, at a workstation LPT1 might be set to refer either to a local printer port or to a remote printer port on a server. Similarly COM1 could be assigned to a local or a remote port.

An important difference between networks is the level at which they allow disk sharing. Some networks share disks at the **drive level**, others allow sharing at the **directory level**. For example, you might want to have access to a particular directory, C:\accounts\data say, and any sub-directories it may have. If the

| Logical Device | Connected to | Physical Device | Operation mode |
|---|---|---|---|
| C | JOHN (001) | HARD1 (C) | Read/Write |
| D | BOB (003) | HARD1 (C) | Read Only |
| E | | | |
| LPT1 | Local | | |
| LPT2 | JOHN (001) | Printer1 (LPT1) | Write Only |
| COM1 | Local | | |

An allocation table showing that that at the local station:
Drive C is station 001's drive C
Drive D is station 003's drive C and
Printer 2 is station 001's printer 1.

network only allows sharing at the drive level then you would have to connect your drive D: to the remote station's drive C: and then change directory to \accounts\data, i.e. CD D:\accounts\data. If the network allows sharing at the directory level then you can simply connect your drive D: to the required directory and from that moment on any reference to D: would be taken to mean \accounts\data on drive C: of the remote station. The advantage of sharing at the directory level is that the user can be restricted to the directory to which the drive letter has been connected. In fact there is no reason why the user should have any knowledge of any other part of the drive. Sharing at the directory level can be achieved in some networks by using the SUBST command or a network equivalent of it. The SUBST command allows a drive letter to be assigned to any directory, local or remote. It is important to notice that the SUBST command isn't supported on some networks.

# NETWORK NAMES

Each workstation on a network must have some method of identifying it uniquely. At the hardware level this is usually by a station number. However at a higher level nearly all networks provide some kind of network naming facility so that users are relieved of the need to remember that network station 134232 has the laser printer connected to it. Some networks allow workstations to be allocated fixed names and some allow the users of the workstations to be named. The advantage of fixed workstation names is that it makes it easy for users to remember the names of the server workstations. The advantage of user names is that different users can log on to a workstation and be automatically connected to a range of network devices that is determined by the name they used to log on.

As well as providing names for workstations and users some networks allow names to be given to shared resources – **share** names. For example, if the directory C:\accounts\data is assigned the share name db then a remote user could connect their drive D: to db without having to know the full name of the directory or even where is was stored. Similarly if LPT1 at a particular server is given the share name laser then a remote workstation could make use of it by connecting LPT1 device to laser. Notice how share names avoid the user having to think in terms of connecting their drive D: to someone else's drive C: or their LPT1 to someone else's LPT1. Share names allow the simplicity of connecting an MS-DOS device to a named resource and offer a network-wide and consistent way of referring to the same resource. (For more information on network naming see the section on **name servers** later in this chapter.)

# *TYPES OF SERVER*

If the role of the requester is fairly straightforward once the device assignments have been sorted out, the possible variations on servers is very complex indeed. There are broadly three classes of server each with their own particular problems:

☐ **Device servers** – these share devices such as disk drives and printers to requesters

☐ **Communications servers** – these provide message sending and receiving facilities on the network

☐ **Management servers** – these provide organisational services such as password management and names for the network stations.

Device servers are the largest and most complex class of server and deserve an extensive discussion. The other two types of server are described later in this chapter.

# DEVICE SERVERS

### DISK SERVERS

The most important type of device server is one that allows multiple users to share a disk drive. Sharing a hard disk is often the main motivation for installing a network. For this reason alone you may be surprised to learn that there are a lot of networks that have very poor disk servers. The reason is that allowing a number of PCs to share a hard disk is very difficult because MS-DOS is a **single user** operating system. In normal operation only one user, and hence one program, can read or write to a hard disk. Connecting a PC to a network changes this by allowing many users and programs to read and write the hard disk at the same time and MS-DOS cannot easily cope with this.

To be more precise there is no real problem as long as all the sharers are reading data from disk. As long as the disk isn't modified in any way then any number of network stations can read its directory information and then the data they need from the areas of the disk where the directory indicates it is stored. If two or more stations are writing to the disk or modifying it in any way then it is very possible that a network station will read directory information that is immediately changed by another station and so act on the basis of a directory that no longer reflects the current state of the disk. For example, a DIR command might show that a file exists but another user might have deleted it in the meantime. Similarly two users might try to write two files with the same name or be allocated the same area of free space on the disk to store their files. These are all situations brought about by the multi-user nature of networking and the single user nature of MS-DOS.

There are three possible solutions:

☐   Restrict the way that the shared disk can be accessed so that the problem goes away.

☐ Change MS-DOS to have some multi-user disk facilities

☐ Abandon MS-DOS in favour of an alternative multi-user operating system

### RESTRICTED ACCESS DISK SERVERS

Many early network operating systems solved the disk sharing problem by **partitioning** the single hard disk into **volumes**, each one behaving like a separate disk drive. Even in a non-networked situation MS-DOS allows a single hard disk to be partitioned so that portions of it can be used for different purposes. For example, you can have two different operating systems, MS-DOS and Unix say, installed on two different partitions of the same disk. Another reason for partitioning a hard disk is that the maximum capacity of disk that MS-DOS (up to Version 3) can handle is 32Mb and so if you have a 40Mb drive one way of using it is to divide it up into two 20Mb partitions – one as drive C: say and the other as drive D:.

Disk partitions formed an obvious and simple way for network extensions to MS-DOS to allow a number of users to access the same disk. Each user is allocated a partition, usually referred to as a **volume** in network jargon, and no-one else is allowed to use the same volume. As MS-DOS is capable of keeping track of operations on a number of different disk drives at the same time there is no need for any great changes to allow one user to access each drive. This approach was used with reasonable success by the pioneering EtherShare system from 3Com. (Note: this method has now been superseded in 3Com's current products.)

The disadvantage of using volumes is that sharing data and applications programs is made more difficult than in the case of the simultaneous sharing of one large volume. There is also the question of how large a volume to assign to each user. If too much disk space is allocated then it goes to waste even though other users might like to use it. Too little and the user is constantly running out of storage. A more serious problem is that if two or more users do choose to share a single volume then there are no problems as long as they simply read data. However if two of the users attempt to write to the disk simultaneously there is a high probability that they will both be allocated the same free area for their file with obvious and disastrous results.

Even though most network operation systems now have better ways of dealing with simultaneous writing to a disk than volumes many still support this feature. The reason is that it can sometimes be useful to allocate a private volume to a workstation. For example, if some workstations have one floppy drive, some two and some none then you could a emulate the missing drives by allocating private volumes to the workstations that needed them. Some networks insist that you allocate a private volume to any workstation that doesn't have any floppy disks at all as a means of getting such workstations started – i.e. the private volume plays the role of their boot disk.

A different sort of restricted access is to be found in low cost networks such as Sagenet. In this case any workstation can read data from the disk of another workstation but cannot write data to it. If data needs to be shared then a copy of the file has to be made on a local storage device. This is clearly a very limited form of disk and data sharing.

## MULTI-USER MS-DOS – FILE SERVERS
Although MS-DOS is a single user operating system it is possible to make it deal with more than one task at a time. In fact every MS-DOS system already has this ability because it supports printer spooling. If you look up the PRINT command in your MS-DOS manual you will discover that you can arrange to print a file while running some other program. What happens is that every time your PC's internal clock ticks it switches its attention from the program you are running to the task of printing the file and then back again

to your program. This switching between two programs is a rudimentary form of multi-tasking known as **foreground/ background** operation. Many network operating systems make use of this foreground/background operation to add a more complex form of multi-tasking to MS-DOS. For example, the 3+ network operating system from 3Com adds two modules to MS-DOS to enhance its multi-tasking – a process manager that decides which task should run next and CIOSYS, a special multi-access disk I/O system. Not all network operating systems go this far and you will find that some are more efficient than others at sharing disks in this way.

Some early networking operating systems added multi-user features to MS-DOS but failed to arrange for the disk to be shared properly. Such networks would seem to operate correctly for most of the time but would occasionally produce errors in the filing system – two files would be stored mixed together or storage would go missing on a hard disk (lost clusters). Fortunately this problem is not common these days but if you suspect a network of being unreliable in this area then try the tests outlined in the technical box.

# TECHNICAL BOX

## CHECKING THAT DISK SHARING WORKS

It is possible that you may come across a network that doesn't implement the sharing of disks correctly. This can still occasionally result in the allocation of the same disk cluster to two different files. The problem for the network buyer is that it can be very difficult to discover exactly how a network handles the disk sharing problem. A network that is sufficiently in tune with current standards to claim to be MS-DOS Version 3 or PC LAN compatible will usually be safe to use – but it is best to check before you trust it.

If you have access to a demonstration network then it is easy to test that the disk sharing is workable. First run CHKDSK to see what the state of the hard disk is before the experiment. Deal with any problems, such as lost clusters or cross linked files, so that the disk is perfect. Once the hard disk is known to be in good condition simply arrange for two workstations to be connected to the same disk server and use the MS-DOS copy command to copy two large files to the same shared directory, one file from each workstation, at the same time. To check that the disk sharing has worked run the MS-DOS FC (File Compare) command to see if both copies are the same as their originals. It is also worth running CHKDSK to see if it reports that the files are cross linked. If it does then the same free cluster was allocated to both files. If it reports cross linkage of files that weren't involved in the test then this is probably due to some disk fault that occurred in the past. Another problem to check for is the creation of lost clusters caused by the fragmentation of the free chain during simultaneous file creation. This too can be recognised by CHKDSK reporting lost clusters.

Once you have tried this basic test you can see how your network copes with more complex situations. Try three workstations copying files at the same time – although if the disk sharing works with two stations it will tend to work with more. Repeat the test with the server acting as one of the workstations copying files. It is not impossible for the network software to treat the server differently (and perhaps incorrectly) from the other workstations. You can also try the effect of switching off one of the workstations while they are both copying. The file corresponding to the workstation that was switched off should be lost but the other files should be saved correctly.

# ALTERNATIVE OPERATING SYSTEMS

One approach to the problem of MS-DOS not being a multi-user operating system is to simply abandon MS-DOS in favour of a true multi-user operating system. The difficulty with this approach is that changing operating systems is a big upheaval. Users have to be retrained and applications programs generally have to be changed. Clearly the only sort of change that can really be contemplated is to an operating system that can emulate MS-DOS very closely.

This approach was taken by Novell when they produced the Netware operating system. They re-wrote MS-DOS 3.1 to give it all of the capabilities that a network operating system needs. The only problem with Netware is that it uses a different disk format to MS-DOS and this means that existing hard disks have to be re-formatted. The benefit of this re-write of MS-DOS is that Netware offers the highest performance disk servers available. Netware is almost an industry standard for high performance networking operating systems but is has to be kept in mind that it is only an emulation of MS-DOS and so there may be problems running some applications packages – no-one can guarantee that an emulation will behave exactly like the real thing. Notice however that this objection vanishes if the disk server is dedicated to its task. Then there is no need at all for it to be in the slightest bit MS-DOS compatible!

A slightly different approach is to use an operating system like Concurrent DOS or CDOS which is an existing multi-tasking operating system that looks to the user a lot like MS-DOS with additional facilities. CDOS will also run most existing MS-DOS applications programs without any change. The advantage of using an existing multi-tasking/user operating system is that it already has many of the facilities needed to deal with multi-user applications. (See Chapter 4 for a discussion of **resource locking**.) This means that any multi-user application that is written to work under CDOS should work immediately without any changes on a network based on CDOS.

To take advantage of this Digital Research, the writers of CDOS, have produced DR NET. This allows workstations running CDOS, CP/M 86, MP/M and DOS Plus to work on the same network. Disk servers have to be running CDOS but requester workstations can use DOS Plus say if required. DR NET shares a disk by running **shadow processes** on the server for each remote station connected to it.

The shadow process is responsible for making the disk requests to CDOS on behalf of the requester. In this way, from the server's point of view there is little difference between a program being run on the server workstation and one on a remote workstation – they are simply examples of the multiple tasks that it has to manage. As now each remote station can itself be running more than one applications program – remember CDOS is truly multitasking – the only complication is that the server might have to run more than one shadow process for each workstation connected to it. In fact it has to run one shadow process for each task on each workstation connected to it and in this sense it is better to think in terms of the different tasks being connected to a server rather than to the workstation that they are running on. For example, CDOS allows the user a number of virtual screens each one capable of running a different program. It is quite permissible in DR NET for one of the screens to be connected to a server, as drive C: say, and another screen to be using the local drive as drive C: at the same time! This has the potential to be confusing to the user unless properly organised but it is a very powerful idea.

# *TECHNICAL BOX*

## THE EVOLUTION OF DISK SERVERS

Systems that employ private volumes as their sole method of controlling simultaneous access are usually referred to as **disk servers**. A disk server allows the copy of MS-DOS in each workstation to handle all of the work necessary to look after the filing system. This means that the workstation sends requests to the disk server to read or write a particular disk sector or cluster. Because the information about which clusters are to be read or written is held locally there is no way that the requester or the server can be aware of what multiple users of the same disk may be doing. This means that it is possible for the same free clusters to be used by different workstations to store files.

### File servers
The next stage in the development of disk servers is the introduction of **file servers**. A file server workstation accepts the responsibility for deciding which particular disk clusters will be used to store any particular file. In other words the disk allocation is centralised within the file server and the remote workstations can only ask it to supply or create a file by giving its name rather than location on disk. File servers have the obvious advantage over simple disk servers in that disk allocation collisions cannot occur due to different requester workstations trying to use the same free area of the disk.

### Application servers
The current generation of file servers are workable in the sense that they allow multiple users to share the same disk but in many applications they are extremely inefficient in terms of their use of the network. For example, imagine a network with a standard file server holding a central database and a remote workstation trying to find say one record that meets some criterion. As the database application is being run on the remote workstation there is no way that the file server can select the records and so every single record in the database has to be transmitted to the remote station to be processed. To have to transmit perhaps thousands of records over the network so that the remote can find just one is clearly inefficient. A better solution would be to have the server act as a **database server**. In this case the remote workstation would simply specify the criterion that the required record had to satisfy and then wait for the database server to locate it and transmit it over the network. At the moment there are no low cost database servers but this is certain to change in the near future as a number of database companies have announced that they are working on products. In the same way that a database server deals with remote workstations at a level that needs some understanding of the application, so it is possible to imagine other **applications servers** that not only supply data but do some of the work of the application. Once again such applications servers do not exist at present but they are a natural and inevitable development.

| Physical Device Name | Access Rights by Password | | Access Rights by User ID |
|---|---|---|---|
| Floppy 1 | | | [255,255] -,-,- |
| Hard 1 | ABC | W | [200,100] W,W,R |
| Printer 1 | ABC | W | |

Access rights table set by server giving:
no access to floppy 1
read/write access to hard 1 using password ABC,
to user group 200 and user 100
read only access to all other users
read/write access to printer 1 using password ABC

---

# PRINTER SERVERS

The simplest sort of printer server merely allows remote workstations to 'connect' to its printer port. Obviously there has to be some way of controlling access to a printer to avoid multiple use. Many networks do not bother to provide automatic protection and rely on the users agreeing who can use the printer at any given time.

A more sophisticated type of printer server is based on the idea of spooling. In this system each workstation sends its data to the printer server which stores it on disk in readiness for sending to the printer. Each file in the print queue is sent to the printer in turn. This is obviously an extension of the usual MS-DOS printer spooling via the PRINT command. Networks differ in the speed with which print files are dealt with and the facilities that they offer to control the print queue. In particular, some allow priorities to be assigned to the files in the print queue that determine the order in

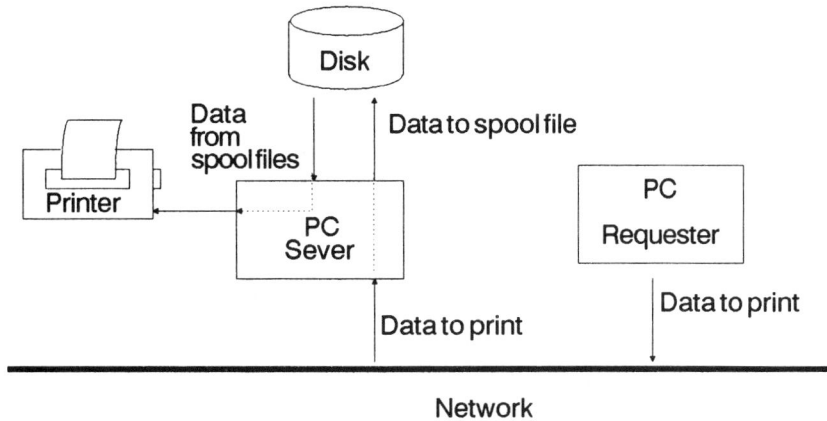

## Printer spooling

which they are sent to the printer. Other networks simply allow the user of the printer server to delete and alter the order of files in the print queue.

A particular problem with using printer spooling on a network is how the printer server knows that a remote machine has finished sending data and that the resulting file should be printed. You might think that simply waiting for the stream of data from the remote to stop would be sufficient but how does the remote machine know that it isn't just a pause before more data is sent. Applications programs often generate printer output in fits and starts. If you can guarantee that no data transmitted for $t$ seconds is a sure sign that the applications program has finished then you can set up the printer server so that it closes the file and adds it to the queue if a no data is received for $t$ seconds. This is often referred to as a **timeout**. The only problem with this method is that the remote station's output has to wait for $t$ seconds before it even has a chance of being printed. A better method is to insist that every workstation sends an end-of-print signal when it has finished. This can be done automatically by the application program if it has this capability or manually by way of a special network command.

Printer spooling can generally cope with both parallel and serial printers. This means that nothing extra is generally required to drive plotters and other serial output devices over a network.

# MODEM SERVERS

Support for modem sharing is relatively limited on most low cost networks. Some will allow one remote station at a time to connect to a serial port in much the same way as the simplest printer server allows a remote to connect to a parallel port.

More sophisticated modem servers that allow more than one user access are not really possible because, except in very special circumstances, modems are not shareable. The best that can be achieved is typified by NosTalk for the Corvus network which will queue users' requests to use the modem and inform them when it is free.

# COMMUNICATIONS SERVERS

### INTERACTIVE COMMUNICATIONS
All networks allow some kind of inter-station messaging. The most rudimentary type of messaging is the direct communication between two or more stations that are actually switched on and connected to the network. For example, ON-LINE CHAT for use with the D-Link network allows one station to select up to three users from the list of current users. Each user is then automatically asked if they agree to chat. If they do they are allocated an area of

the screen where their messages are displayed. In this way up to four people can have an interactive conversation using the network as the communications channel. This sort of communications is sometimes useful if the physical distance between workstations is large. It can also be useful if one network user wants to pass messages to another user while on the phone or while unable to talk openly.

**E-MAIL**

Inter-station E-mail is more complicated than interactive chatting because of the need to use a server to collect and distribute mail to workstations as they log on. The mail server has to know who the mail is for and be able to store it in a temporary location until it can be delivered. This is very similar to printer spooling. The only really difficult part of the E-mail server is how it knows who the message is for and this is often something that needs the co-operation of a name server – see below.

# MANAGEMENT SERVERS

This is one area where networks differ greatly. Some have a range of management servers others have virtually none, relying instead on each workstation looking after its own affairs. Three examples of management servers are:

☐  network synchronisers

☐  name servers

☐  permissions servers

# NETWORK SYNCHRONISERS

Although many PCs have real time clocks that keep the correct time even when the machine is switched off, it is desirable that all computers on the network show the same time. The reason for this is that otherwise the time and date stamp that a file receives might depend on who created it or there might be a discrepancy between the time and date stamped and that shown on the remote machine. A **network synchroniser** or **time server** is simply a workstation that will supply the time and date to each workstation as it is turned on and connected (in the software sense) to the network. Another alternative is that the time server transmits the time in response to the heart beat signals that each workstation sends out to indicate to the network servers that it is still logged on to the network. In this way a standard network time can be established and maintained. Notice that for obvious reasons there can only be one synchroniser on any one network!

# NAME SERVERS

Every station on the network has to have a unique station number, address or node number. Although from the network hardware and software point of view this number is sufficient to distinguish one machine from another, and so to decide for whom a packet of data is intended, it is very off-putting for the user to have to refer to say station 1233280. In practice it is more convenient to assign names to each workstation so that one user can send a message to PETE, JOHN or ACCOUNTS rather than to meaningless addresses. Obviously the network software has to somehow decode these network names to the correct network addresses. There are two main ways of doing this – centrally at a single workstation or **name server** or locally at each workstation.

For example, if a name server is established so that it has a pre-prepared list of names and their corresponding station numbers that it can read from disk then each workstation can request these names as it logs on to the network. This means that a name server supplies a fixed and network-wide list of names. The alternative is to allow each user to log on to the network with a specific network name. For example, if PETE logs on at station 6 then from that moment on station 6 remembers that its name is PETE. Other stations discover this fact by simply asking all the workstations on the network to broadcast their name in turn. In this way a network-wide system of names can be maintained but it isn't necessarily a fixed list and names might move with their user from one station to another. This is not a bad situation from the point of view of the requester workstations because their identity should only determine their access rights to the network resources and these rights shouldn't vary from one workstation to another. However from the point of the server workstations continuously changing names can be something of a problem. Imagine one day having to connect to a disk drive or printer on PETE's machine, only to discover a few hours later that it was now JOHN's. Even if dynamic naming is possible in a network there is no need to make use of it and the problem is solved by insisting that all server stations have fixed names. (That is all server stations should log on to the network using the autoexec.bat file which always uses the same log on name.)

# PERMISSIONS SERVERS

There is a need in any network to determine and control what users or workstations have access to. As in the case of the name server this facility can be provided centrally or distributed over the network. For example, some networks use an extended name server to record passwords for logging on and for access to the various shared resources on the network. Access to disks is usually controlled at a number of different levels. A network user may be given permission to read a disk, or to read and write a disk. It may also be possible to restrict users to particular sub-directories. For example, a user may be able to read and write files in one sub-directory but only read files in another. It is also possible for a certain amount of protection to be given to files by setting them to Read Only status using the MS-DOS command ATTRIB. Of course it is quite possible for a remote user to use the ATTRIB command to unprotect a file if they have read/write access over the network to the disk so this is only protection against accidental modification.

The alternative to using a central permissions server is for each network station to maintain their own password and permissions list. It is obviously simple for each station to keep a list of its possible users and their associated passwords. This scheme implies that it is possible to restrict the workstations from which any particular user can log on to the network. Similarly it is also easy for each network server to keep a list of passwords and access permissions. For example, the D-Link network creates a file called name.LGN for each user name which stores the password necessary for that user to be allowed to log on and a two-part identity number which controls the user's access rights. The two-part identity number is made up of a three-digit group number and a three-digit user number. Server stations can be set up so that they allow different access rights according to group number and user number. For example, a server might give read/write access to all group 200 users and read only access to the rest.

# FILE SHARING

Even if a network correctly implements a disk server that allows users to share a disk without any errors due to the accidental allocation of the same area of free disk space there are still problems to be solved. In particular it is not desirable for more than one user to be able to modify a file at the same time. This is the **simultaneous update problem** and its solution is essential if a network is going to offer its users the possibility of sharing data as well as hardware. You could say that the ability to share disk hardware is a prerequisite for sharing data but you still need to add some controls on how the data is shared to make sure that it happens in an orderly fashion. Most networks solve this problem by a system of **resource locks** which are used to indicate to other network users when a resource such as a file or a record in a database is being used. Locking is an important topic for the correct running of most network applications programs and it is covered in the next chapter.

# *SUMMARY*

- Workstations can either be servers, requesters or a mixture of both.

- Servers can be dedicated or non-dedicated (i.e. used like a normal workstation).

- It is better if servers are based on more powerful 286 or 386 machines.

- Networks can be homogeneous, single server or mixed. Single server networks are the simplest from the user's viewpoint.

- Requesters can use services by connecting their local drive or device identifiers to the remote devices offered for sharing.

- Shared resources can identified by their own workstation's drive or device identifier or can be given a share name.

- Disk servers are implemented either by allocating a disk volume for each user, adding multi-tasking modules to MS-DOS or by replacing MS-DOS by a compatible multi-tasking operating system.

- Print servers share the seemingly unshareable by using printer spooling.

- Communications servers can offer instantaneous message passing, on line chatting or full E-mail facilities.

- Network management servers look after share names, user names, time service and access rights.

# 4. Single User Applications

Although one of the biggest benefits of installing a network is the sharing of data and the automatic interaction between users that this brings about, the most immediate benefit is the sharing of existing single user applications. It is usual for a number of individual PCs to have been in operation before the installation of the network for applications such as word processing, spreadsheet and limited database. Once a network is installed it is natural to transfer these applications to network operation and allow each user of a workstation the benefits of the same programs that were in use before the network. This is an excellent idea because the people who were using the applications packages would resist any attempt at changing to some other package and they possess a bank of existing knowledge and experience of those packages that ought not to be discarded without considering the cost.

The only problem with this approach is that the applications programs that were in use before the network was installed are almost certainly going to be single user packages and the network is an inherently multi-user environment. While in nearly all cases this will not stop you from using the single user applications, it can cause the occasional problem if two users attempt to work with the same files at the same time.

In this chapter we take a look at the problems of single user software on a network and examine the solutions. Perhaps surprisingly, most of the solutions depend on using facilities provided by MS-DOS Version 3.1, 3.2, 3.3 or subsequent (referred to collectively as V3.x) and if there is a single message contained in this chapter it is that MS-DOS V3.x is the networking standard for applications software.

# SHARING FILES

Obviously it is important that a network implements disk and file sharing in such a way that the contents of the disk or file are not damaged by normal operations. This is usually described as ensuring the **integrity** of the filing system. We have already looked in Chapter 3 at one way that network operation can damage the integrity of the filing system if steps are not taken to avoid the allocation of the same free disk space to different workstations, but this is not the only type of problem. Even if you assume a correctly constructed network that will allow multiple users to share a disk drive with no problems there are still difficulties if users choose to share the same file. For example, if two users on different workstations read the same copy of a document into their word processors, modify it in different ways and then save it back to disk – which modification if any will be stored?

The simultaneous file update problem isn't a new one. It has occurred ever since computers were first used by multiple users. In other words, many of the problems that are now being encountered by network users were encountered and solved by the multi-user operating systems of the sixties. The basic idea introduced then was the use of **locks** to control access to each shareable resource. A lock is simply used to signal that a resource is already in use and any other user wanting access to it should wait until the resource is **unlocked**.

User A locks the file
before making changes
to it.

User B tries to make changes
to the file

STOP!
File locked.

File

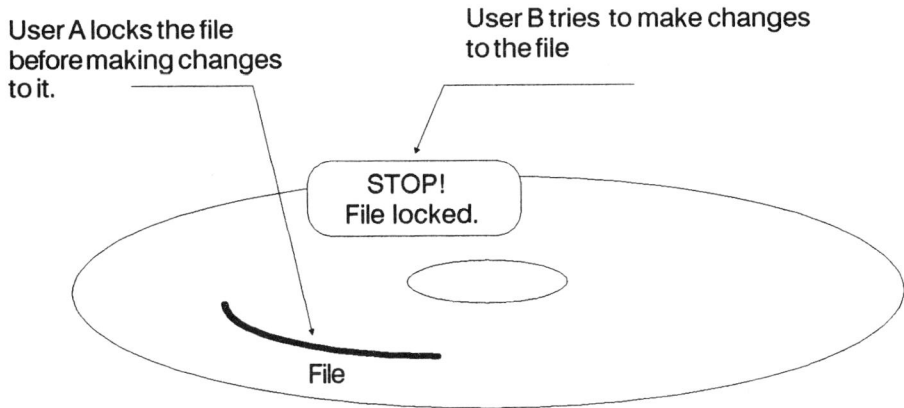

If the file is locked before user A tries to work with it then the simultaneous update problem vanishes because only one user can work with it at a time.

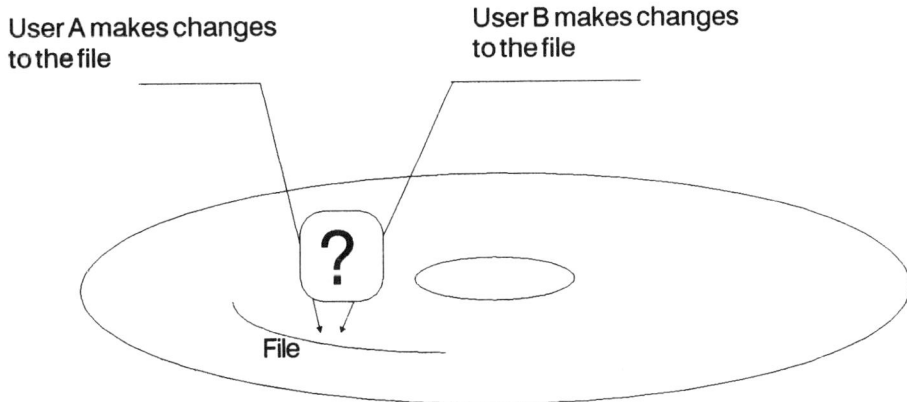

User A makes changes
to the file

User B makes changes
to the file

?

File

The simultaneous update problem. If user A and user B try to change a file at the same time then which changes survive depend on who writes the file last!

There are two types of resource locking encountered in practice – **coercive** or **physical locking** and **logical locking**. In physical locking a subsequent user trying to get at the resource is automatically denied access and cannot get at it even if it wants to ignore the lock and proceed, regardless of the consequences. A logical lock is more a 'gentleman's agreement' that before accessing any resource then the program will check the state of the lock and not access the resource if it is free. Of course any program is able to ignore or not even bother to test for a logical lock and so in theory simultaneous access is still possible. In practice a logical lock is as good as a physical lock as long as all the software working on the network is well-behaved. Indeed the physical locks offered by a network are often so limited that applications software either implements a second system of logical locking or even uses the physical locking to implement logical locking.

# SEMAPHORES

Most locking schemes make use of some kind of 'in-use' indicator or **flag**. The first program to want to use the resource looks at the in-subsequent program tries to make use of the same resource it will find the in-use flag set and wait while until the first user finishes with the resource and resets the flag.

This scheme is simple but it has a serious defect that usually only comes to light after it has been in use for some time. Imagine that two programs want to use a free device at exactly the same moment. They both look at the in-use flag at roughly the same time (one immediately after the other) and discover that it isn't set so they both decide to set it and use the resource! This problem arises because the operation of testing and setting of the flag occurs in two separate steps. If the test and set operation were to be performed as one single indivisible operation then the problem would vanish. For example, if two programs attempt to use the same resource at

User A looks at flag and finds
the resource free

User B looks at flag before A has
had time to set it and so finds
the resource free

**FREE**

**FREE**

Resource controlled by
flag

(Printer, file, modem etc.)

Resource controlled by
flag

(Printer, file, modem etc.)

User A now sets the flag
and starts using
the resource

User B also sets the flag
and starts using
the resource

**IN USE**

**IN USE**

Resource controlled by
flag now in use by A

(Printer, file, modem etc.)

Resource controlled by
flag now in use by A & B!

(Printer, file, modem etc.)

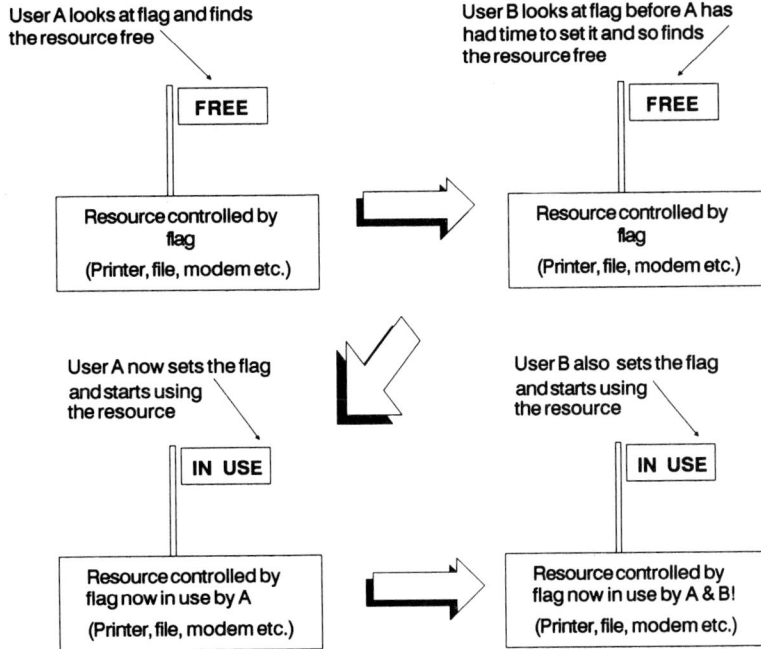

The failure of the flag

Because testing and setting a flag are two operations it is possible for user B to
test the flag before A has managed to set it and so they both end up using a
resource that only one should be allowed to use at a time.

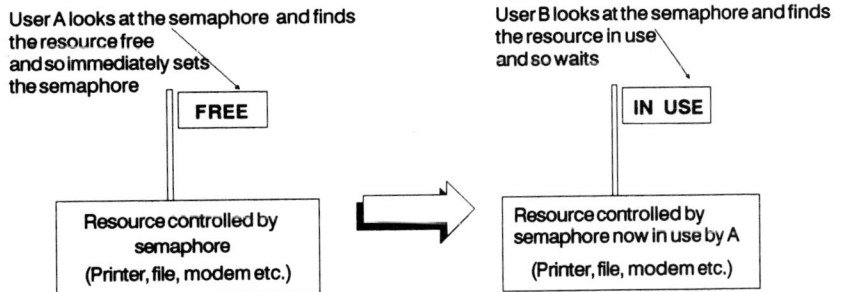

User A looks at the semaphore and finds
the resource free
and so immediately sets
the semaphore

User B looks at the semaphore and finds
the resource in use
and so waits

**FREE**

**IN USE**

Resource controlled by
semaphore

(Printer, file, modem etc.)

Resource controlled by
semaphore now in use by A

(Printer, file, modem etc.)

A semaphore has to be tested and set in one operation. This stops the
simultaneous use of a resource no matter how soon B tries to test the
semaphore.

exactly the same time one of them will test the flag and then immediately set the flag before the other looks at it. A flag that is used with this sort of test and set operation is generally referred to as a **semaphore**. Many networks provide semaphores or use semaphores as the basis of their locking system but you should be aware of the sloppy terminology used in many networks.

# THE DEADLY EMBRACE

The **deadly embrace** is a well known problem in computer science and it can arise with surprising ease. For example, if two network users both need access to file A and B then a deadly embrace can result if they each attempt to lock the files in a different order. For example, if one program opens and locks file A and the other opens and locks file B then there is no problem. If the first program then

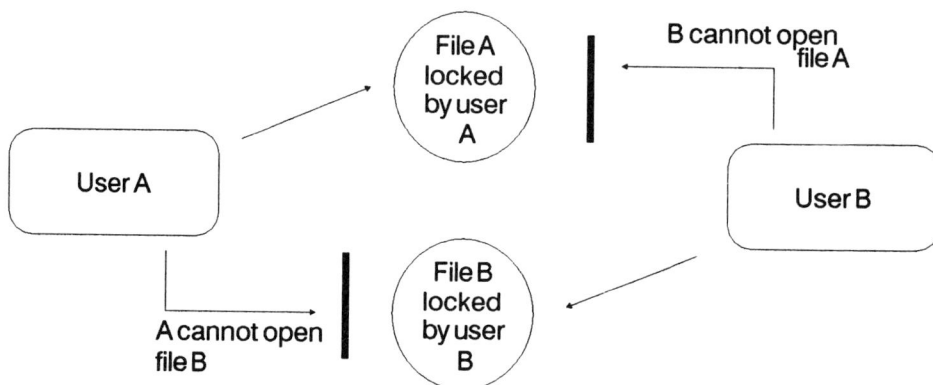

The deadly embrace - A waits for B to finish and B waits for A to finish!

tries to open file B it will find it locked and so it has to wait. The second program, the one that owns file B, then tries to open file A but it finds it locked and so waits for it to become free. Neither of the programs has the benefit of our overview and so they both wait for each other to release the file that they need to finish. It is obvious that unless something intervenes each program will wait forever – hence deadly embrace!

You need not worry too much about the deadly embrace as it is something that programmers do try to avoid in producing applications programs. For example in practice the two programs described above would open the files in the same order, i.e. file A followed by file B and so the deadly embrace described would not occur. However it is worth being aware of the possibility of a deadly embrace arising in a network. If you do discover such a problem the easiest solution is to simply abort one of the two programs which allows the other to continue. The deadly embrace can arise in ways that involve more than two programs, for example:

Program 1 wants to use file A and has locked file B

Program 2 wants to use file B and has locked file C

Program 3 wants to use file C and has locked file A

is a three program deadly embrace, however such things are rare in practice.

## DIRECTORY LOCKING

The most fundamental and in some ways least useful form of locking is **directory locking**. Most networks, but by no means all, allow the network manager to decide not only which disk drives will be shared but which directories will be shared. In most cases directories can be established as private or shared and it is not difficult to see that any single user application can be run

```
                        C:\ (root)
            _____/  |  _____
           /       |      |              \
        GEM     MSDOS    APPS          UTILITIES
                        /  \            /    \
                      WP    SP       DIAG  BACKUP
                     /
                  BOOK
                     \
                    LETTERS
```

Access to \APPS\WP restricts
the user to WP and its sub-directories

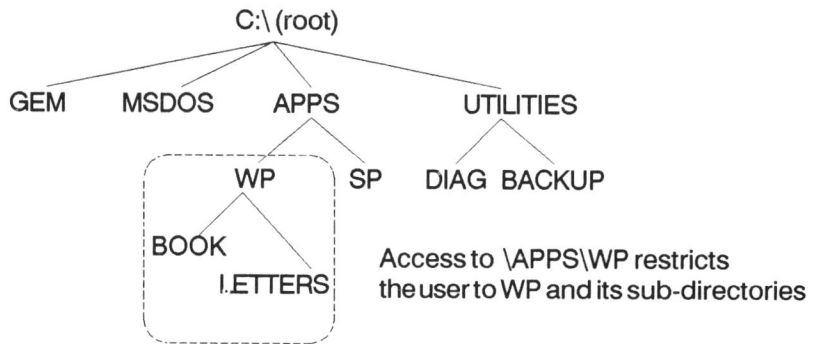

Directory locking

successfully on a network if both the program and the data reside in private or single user access directories. The reason is simply that using private directories in this way mimics the single user MS-DOS environment. Of course if this is the way that a program has to be run then you lose the potential advantages of a network but it can be useful for highly specialised programs that are simply running on the network to make use of resource sharing.

Notice that networks do not enforce any sort of automatic directory locking. Which directories are shared and which private is something that has to be determined by the network manager, or more specifically each disk server, during the configuration of the network. The access rights to a directory generally work in such a way that they also apply to all lower sub-directories. That is, if you share the directory APP/WP then you will also share any sub-directories of APP/WP but not any of those higher in the directory structure, i.e. not APP and not the root, etc...

# MS-DOS V3.x AND LOCKING

When MS-DOS V3.x was introduced it contained a number facilities to implement file locking. This might appear a strange addition to a single user operating system – after all locking is only necessary where there is the possibility of more than one user accessing a resource! Of course the explanation behind this seeming paradox was that they were intended to support multi-user access in a network environment – MS-NET and PC LAN to be precise. Strangely the MS-DOS V3.x locking facility has now become a standard for true multi-user MS-DOS compatible operating systems such as Concurrent DOS from DR. This means that multi-user applications programs written to run under any LAN that makes use of MS-DOS V3.x locking should also work on Concurrent DOS and vice versa. In other words, MS-DOS V3.x is fast becoming a standard for all multi-user applications, irrespective of whether they are to be running on a network or under a multi-user operating system.

Surprisingly it is also possible for file locks to be important in a stand-alone single user system. Many MS-DOS applications allow users to run an MS-DOS command while they are still active. For example, if you are editing a file in WordStar V4 you can press Ctrl/F to produce a screen display that offers you the chance to run an MS-DOS command. Of course while you are running such a command the document that you were editing is open and still in use and there is the possibility that you might try to modify it using commands such as erase, copy, etc. In this case file locking might just manage to stop you from doing something silly. A more general example of this is provided by the ability that Windows offers users to open multiple screen windows, each with a different application running. Although only one window is active at any given moment it is still possible for the application in the active window to try to modify a file already in use by an application in a suspended window. Once again MS-DOS file locking would stop this from being a problem.

Clearly the way that MS-DOS V3.x implements locks is important but some network operating systems use their own system of locks or supplement the MS-DOS V3.x locks. In the main these differences only become important while running true multi-user software such as database programs which allow simultaneous access. In this chapter we take a look at simple MS-DOS V3.x locking and some of the extensions necessary to take care of all the possibilities that occur in practice. It is also important to note that MS-DOS doesn't enforce any of the directory locking or more complex access schemes described earlier. It only locks files and, as we shall see in the next chapter, records.

# MS-DOS V3.x DEFAULT FILE LOCKING

Under MS-DOS V3.x any file that is opened for reading or writing is immediately locked and so all other users are denied access. The lock remains in force until the file is closed and so this should in theory at least restrict access to one user per file at all times. Notice that this default locking will occur even if the program was written to work with the earlier MS-DOS Version 2 as the default locking facility was added to the normal MS-DOS open file routine.

This sort of file locking is entirely adequate for any applications program that opens a file, processes it and closes it only when it is finished modifying it. For example, if a word processor keeps a text file open all the time it is being modified and only closes it when the user is completely finished with it then it is impossible for two users to update it at the same time. If a second user tries to edit the file while the first is working with it the second user will get a file sharing error.

The only problem is that many applications programs don't keep a file open all of the time that they are using it. Some open a file, read it into memory and then immediately close the file. Of course this

Application starts                                              Application stops

| | Uses file A | | Uses file B | |
|---|---|---|---|---|

Open A | Close A | Open B | Close B

File A | | File A locked | | | |

File B | | | | File B locked | |

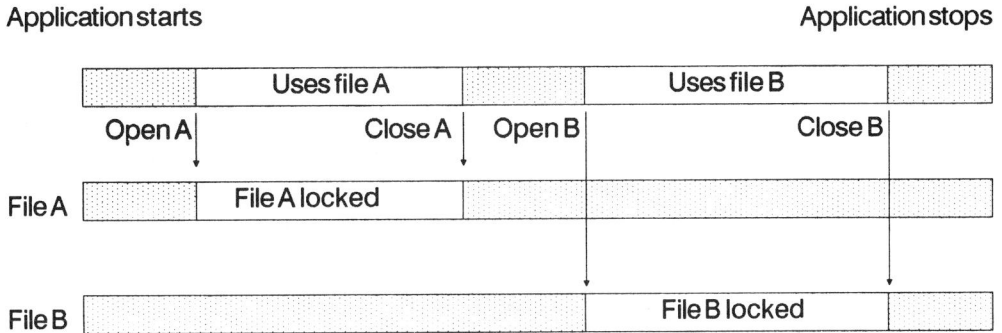

MS-DOS V3.x default file locking

means that a user can modify the contents of the file and then save it back to disk at a later time. It also means that it is possible for two users to edit the same file at the same time as long as they open the file one after the other. To get around this problem explicit, rather than default, file locking has to be used. This is discussed later in this chapter.

# SHARING READ ONLY FILES

Default file locking is something that solves the simultaneous update program by stopping file sharing completely. The only problem is that there are some files, in particular the applications programs themselves, that do need to be shared. As long as a file is only going to be read by the different users there is no danger in sharing it – there can be no simultaneous update because no one updates it. In recognition of this fact MS-DOS V3.x does not lock a file that is set to READ ONLY. You can set any file to read only status using the ATTRIB command –

ATTRIB +R filename

sets the specified file to read only status and

ATTRIB −R filename

restores it to read/write status. You can set a group of files to read only status using MS-DOS wildcards. For example, to set all .EXE programs to READ ONLY you would use –

ATTRIB +R *.EXE

In general it is a good idea to set all the shareable program files to read only status. In practice this means setting all .COM, .EXE and program overlays (usually .OVL) to READ ONLY.

The only problem with setting shared files to read only is that some applications programs actually write to their program or overlay files for security or other reasons and this tends to make the program inherently unshareable.

# PROBLEMS WITH SINGLE USER SOFTWARE

Given a well behaved single user applications program, i.e. one that leaves files open while they are being modified, MS-DOS V3.x default file locking does remove the danger of simultaneous update. However there are other aspects of a single user program that cause problems in a multi-user environment. For example, if a single user program needs to create a temporary file and always uses the same file name in the same directory then this will stop a second user from using the program. Applications programs can be configured to store their temporary files in a specific directory and then it is just a matter of arranging that each user has a suitable private directory.

Application starts                                                                              Application stops

| | Read file from disk | Uses file A | Save file to disk | |

Open A|          Close A |                    Open A|          Close A |

File A | | File A locked | | File A locked | |

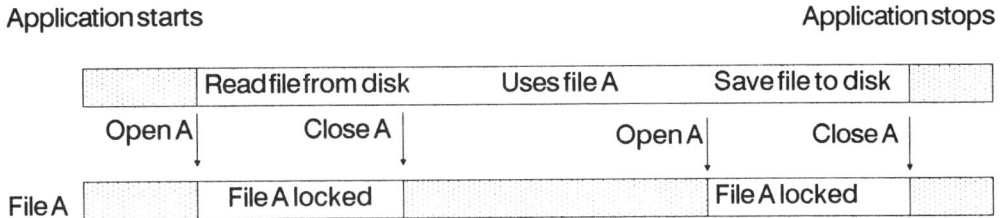

MS-DOS V3.x default file locking can fail to keep a
file locked for the entire time that it is in use

A similar problem arises when the application program reads a
particular file to determine the type of hardware or the directories it
will use. If the PCs attached to the network have different hardware
specifications then there will obviously be a difficulty in running
the same copy of the program on all the workstations. One possible
solution is to provide each user with an individual batch file to get
the application started with the correct configuration but the
practicality of this depends very much on the exact workings of
the program.

A particular problem arises with respect to word processors and
spelling packages. Usually spelling packages come with a ready
made dictionary that is suitable for sharing over the network but
what about the problem of allowing users to add new words? If you
allow everyone to add words then the chances are the dictionary will
become very large and possibly erroneous. A better solution is to
allow each user to add words to their own personal extension to the

dictionary but this implies that the software provides this feature and most single user spelling packages don't – after all why should they in a single user environment?

Copy protection can often mean that a single user program cannot be shared over a network. Many copy protection schemes involve the exact timing of some disk operation or a direct read or write of the disk drive, neither of which work over a network. Of course copy protection is intended to stop people from sharing applications software and so using it over a network probably infringes the licence agreement. In this sense the copy protection is serving its intended function! If you want to use such programs over the network then it is almost certain that you will need to buy a network or multiple user version of the software.

Problems such as these often result in a single user program being difficult and sometimes impossible to share over a network. Usually it isn't easy to detect these operational problems without actually loading and trying an applications program on a network.

# EXPLICIT LOCKING

If an application program is badly behaved and doesn't keep a file open while it is modifying it then MS-DOS V3.x's default locking doesn't stop simultaneous update. Most spreadsheets and a number of word processors work in this way and so it is an important problem. Most networks allow the user to solve the problem by providing either explicit lock and unlock commands or by providing a deferred unlock mode of operation.

The explicit locking commands are the most common. For example, in the Corvus network software PC/NOS there are two

| | | | | | |
|---|---|---|---|---|---|
| Application starts | | | | | Application stops |

| | Read file from disk | Uses file A | Save file to disk | |
|---|---|---|---|---|

Open A | Close A | Open A | Close A |

File A     File A locked

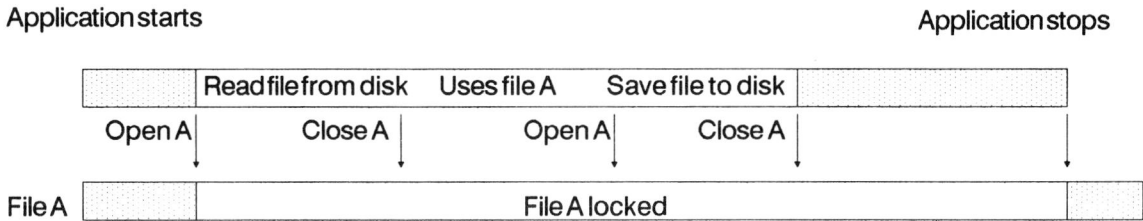

Extended locking keeps a file locked for longer than it is in use
by only unlocking it when the application stops running

commands concerned with locking –

FILELOCK filename EXCL

locks the file for exclusive use and

FILELOCK filename MA

unlocks the file. To test to see if a file is already locked you can use

FILELOCK filename

which lists the lock state of the file and the user who locked it. The
obvious problem with explicit file locking is that the user has to
remember to lock a file before using it and unlock it when finished.
It might be possible to arrange for a batch file to partially automate
the task but it still isn't convenient.

A slightly better method is provided by D-Link's deferred locking
scheme. This is an extension of the MS-DOS V3.x default locking

scheme that keeps a file locked until the application program that opened it terminates. Files that are to be treated as deferred locking files can be set by using the LOCKATR command which reads in a list of file specifications. Default locking is almost automatic but it does mean that a file can be locked for a much longer time than is actually necessary. For example, if a spreadsheet program opens a file first thing in the morning it could remain locked until the end of the day even though it was only used for a few moments!

Explicit locking is also important because it was the only method of controlling simultaneous access to files in networks that pre-date MS-DOS V3.x. These early networks offered a general system of semaphores that users could set and test as needed. This would usually be based on two commands like LLOCK name and UNLOCK name. The LLOCK (LoopLOCK) command would try to lock the semaphore name. If name wasn't already locked it would succeed in locking it and return control to the user. If name was already locked then it would wait (or loop) until it was unlocked (by another user giving the UNLOCK command) and then lock it and return control to the user. As long as all the users of a network agreed to use LLOCK before using any shared resource then only one user could gain access to it at a time. It is important to notice that the name used for the semaphore had no special meaning or association with a resource. For example, as long as all the users of the networks agreed to use a semaphore name X to access the printer say then LLOCK X and UNLOCK X would work as well as a more meaningful name such as LLOCK PRINTER and UNLOCK PRINTER. As long as all the users agree to use the same semaphore names to control access to a device, file or directory then it doesn't matter what it is. Apart from the problem of explicit locking for badly behaved single user applications semaphores are slowly disappearing from the users' view of networking, even if they are still being used beneath the surface.

# SHARED PROGRAMS BUT PRIVATE DATA

A simpler solution to sharing single user applications, and in many cases one which suits the situation quite well, is to use separate directories for the data belonging to each user. In this way the program files can be shared but the data kept well separated. As long as the application program can be set to use a specific drive and/or directory for its data files then implementing separate directories for each use is simple. For example, if you set Lotus 1-2-3 to save its data in D:\LOTUSDATA (using the /Worksheet Global Default Directory command) then each workstation can connect a different drive or directory as their drive D:. This can be achieved either by connecting drive D: to the appropriate directory in networks that share disks at the directory level or by using the standard MS-DOS SUBST command. (Note: the SUBST command cannot be used on some networks which generally provide their own network version.) The SUBST command allows any drive letter to be assigned to a sub-directory residing anywhere in the system. For example, following the command

SUBST D: C:\WORK1

any reference to drive D: will cause files to be stored on drive C: in directory WORK1. Notice that there is nothing stopping drive C: being a remote drive provided by the network disk server. Clearly in this case each workstation would have to use the SUBST command to assign drive D: to a different private directory.

A much simpler situation than this results if each workstation stores data files on a local disk drive – say floppy drive A:. Then there is no need to carry out the SUBST command as long as the application is set to store all its data files in drive A:.

The key to understanding what is going on in each of these cases is to notice that, although the applications program is set to use the same drive or directory name, this is connected to a different drive or directory depending on the workstation.

# MS-DOS V3.x PROGRAMS – EXTENDED LOCKING

The nice thing about MS-DOS V3.x's default locking scheme is that it provides a measure of protection for many programs that were not written with network use in mind. Indeed many were not even written with MS-DOS V3.x in mind. For example, you can take a copy of an old word processor and often use it on a network without the worry that two or more users might edit the same file. If a user does attempt to edit a file while it is in use then they might get a strange error message suggesting that a disk error has occurred rather than a network problem but apart from this it should work as well as a specially written network program.

This said it is worth adding that MS-DOS V3.x does have some additional features that specially written programs can take advantage of. For example there is a new facility that can be used by an application program to create a temporary file with a unique name. Which name is actually used is decided by MS-DOS V3.x but this doesn't matter to the application program as it is only using the file for temporary storage!

Perhaps the most important change is that programs specially written for MS-DOS V3.x can specify the type of use that they are going to be making of a file that they are about to open and what sort of sharing they can tolerate. This means that the simple default file locking provided by MS-DOS V3.x is extended to a range of more subtle locking condition. To be precise an applications program can now open a file for any of the following operations:

☐ Read-Only

☐ Write-Only

☐ Read/Write

and specify the following sharing modes:

☐ lock the file for any subsequent operation
(i.e. exclusive use of the file is requested)

☐ lock for a subsequent read operation
(i.e. no other program can read the file at the same time)

☐ lock for a subsequent write operation
(i.e. no other program can read the file at the same time)

☐ do not lock the file at all
(i.e. allow anyone to share the file)

What happens when a second workstation tries to open a file that is already being used depends on the access and sharing mode used to open the file and the access and sharing mode being requested. It is relatively easy to work out if a subsequent file open will be allowed simply asking if the open would violate any existing locks or try to impose a lock that would make an existing use illegal. For example, if the file is already open for reading with no lock set and a second user requests to read the file with exclusive use the second open will be denied.

Clearly as applications programs start to make use of MS-DOS V3.x's extended file locking facilities the true data sharing potential of networks will be realised.

# SOFTWARE LICENCES

From a user's point of view it is an unfortunate fact that software has to be paid for. Most single user applications programs are sold only with a single user licence. Although the terms of such licences vary, most amount to restricting the use of the software to a single user on a single machine at a single site. Some (for example Borland) allow the user and the site to change as long as only one copy of the software is running at any given moment. In many cases this means that you can install one copy of a program on a network and use it legally as long as only one workstation accesses it at a time. (Note that it is the user's responsibility to check that this is the case.) Conversely this implies that you cannot legally make use of a single copy of a single user program in a true multi-user environment.

It clearly isn't fair to share one copy of a program between ten or twenty users when the manufacturer sets the price assuming that each user would buy one copy. Equally it doesn't seem fair to the user to have to purchase one copy of the program of every workstation on the network because there is no guarantee that every user will want the software. Many software manufacturers are slowly coming round to the point of view that special licensing arrangements are necessary to deal with networks.

The simplest approach, but not well liked by users, is an extension of the standard single licences. In this case the product can be used over a network but a key disk is required for each workstation that wants to make use of the application. This is the scheme used by Lotus 1-2-3 Version 2, for example.

A much better method is the 'X' user licence. In this case the software is licensed for a fixed number of users, irrespective of which workstations are involved. The advantage of this scheme is that any X users on the network can make use of the software. If X+1 users attempt to make use of it then the last one is prohibited until one of the existing users quits the program. dBASE III PLUS uses this scheme, allowing one user for each dBASE III PLUS master disk and five for each LAN pack disk presented to the system.

Another licensing scheme is to licence one copy of the program to the file server. This works because there is very definitely an upper limit to the number of simultaneous users of a file server before the response time becomes too large and a second server is installed.

In practice you will find that each manufacturer has their own variation on one of the licensing schemes described above. The biggest problem that you are likely to encounter is trying to find a reasonable form of licence for a single user program that the manufacturer has never thought of as being capable of running on a network!

# RUNNING REAL SINGLE USER PRODUCTS

At this point you may have decided that the complications of running single user programs on a network are so great that it is an impossibly difficult thing to get right. In practice it isn't so difficult as long as you proceed step by step and try to pin down what is going wrong if anything at each stage. Applications should always be tested from at least two workstations in such a way that the effect of trying to carry out the same operation at the same time can be assessed.

To help you use particular applications packages on a network, notes on the more common packages are listed below. Notice that the absence of a package from the list doesn't imply that there are any known problems in running it on a network. Also notice that some programs are not discussed because they are available in more appropriate LAN versions. In general, databases tend to keep their files open all the time they are being used, word processors vary in their approach and spreadsheets tend to close their files while still working on them.

### dBASE II and III (and dBASE clones)

Sharing data files is beyond the capabilities of a single user database program such as dBASE II and III without a good deal of programming – this is covered in the next chapter. However you can share dBASE II and III code as long as there is no attempt to share datafiles. All versions of dBASE are well behaved and keep files open for the time that they are in use, making default locking sufficient to prevent multiple update. dBASE III PLUS is available in a network form that supports sharing and this is described in the next chapter. Most of the dBASE compatible programs such as Clipper, Foxbase etc. behave in the same way as dBASE.

### Framework I and II

This program closes files while they are still in use and is generally not easy to share. It is better to provide each user with a separate copy.

### GEM Desktop

A single copy of GEM and all GEM applications can be shared on a network with few difficulties as long as all the workstations have the same hardware configuration. The configuration of the system is determined by files stored in the GEMSYS directory on the disk from which GEM is loaded so there seems to be no way to vary the hardware specification from user to user. If there is more than one type of machine connected to the network then each type will have to be given their own copy of GEM.

### Lotus 1-2-3 Version 2.01 and Symphony

These programs present no real problems but spreadsheet files are closed even though they are still being used. The solution is to give each user a private data directory or use local storage for spreadsheets. The programs are copy protected but Lotus will sell additional key disks to allow network use.

### Microsoft Multiplan V3.x

Multiplan V3.x is one spreadsheet that supports network use without any modification or additions. Spreadsheets can be loaded as read only, in which case they are not locked or read/write in which case they are. If a second user tries to load a locked spreadsheet then they are offered the choice of not loading it or loading it just to look at. Multiplan's configuration file MP.INI is loaded from the current directory rather than the directory from which the main program is loaded and so each user can have a different MP.INI file.

### Microsoft Word Version 3

This well known word processor is available in a network version with five user site licences. It is generally recommended that it isn't run on the server that it is installed on. It can make direct use of network printers, share style sheets and stop simultaneous access to documents.

### Paradox Version 2

Make sure that each user has a configuration (.CFG) file in a private directory. Other comments as for dBASE.

### Quattro

Spreadsheet files are closed even though they are still in use. The solution to this is to allocate a data directory or local device to each user for spreadsheet storage. Quattro is not copy protected so running multiple copies is easy.

### SuperCalc Versions 2, 3.x and 4

Spreadsheet files are closed even though they are still in use. The solution to this is to allocate a data directory or local device to each user for spreadsheet storage. SuperCalc is not copy protected so running multiple copies is easy but notice that SuperCalc 4 supports networking and is available in an X user licence form.

**Volkswriter Deluxe Version 2.2**
Use CONFIGUR to set the spill (temporary) files to be on a local or non-shared directory or drive. Also keep data files in separate devices or directories.

**Wordperfect 4.2**
For multi-user use it is essential that the temporary work files are stored in a separate sub-directory for each user. This can be achieved by setting the environment variable WP.

**WordStar Professional 4**
This has built-in support for networking because, for every document, it creates two temporary files called filename.$A$ and filename.$B$. If a second user attempts to edit the file the existence of these temporary files is taken to mean that someone else is using the file. In this case WordStar will allow the second user to look at the file in protected mode but not edit it. It is also possible to share the main dictionary and set the directory that the personal dictionary is to be found in so making it possible for each user to have a different personal dictionary. WordStar has to be informed that it is being used in a multi-user environment during its installation.

# SUMMARY

■ To avoid the simultaneous updating of files a locking scheme has to be used to restrict access to one user at a time.

■ Locking schemes are usually implemented by semaphores even if these are not made visible to the user.

■ The presence of locking raises the possibility of a deadly embrace between multiple users competing for the same resource.

■ Single user applications need locking facilities either at the directory or file level.

■ MS-DOS V3.x implements a default file locking scheme whereby any Read/write file that is opened is locked but a read only file is not locked.

■ As well as the simultaneous update problem there are many other potential difficulties in running single user software on a multi-user network – including clashes between temporary files with the same name, the need for different configuration files, personal dictionaries and copy protection.

■ Some single user programs close a file before they have finished using it. This leaves the file unlocked even though in use and allows the possibility of simultaneous update. This can be solved by explicit locking or deferred locking.

■ Programs that have been written to run under MS-DOS V3.x can make use of an extended range of file locking and other network features. Such programs are clearly to be preferred for network use.

■ Even though it many be possible to run a single user program on a network it is important to check that this is not breaking the single user licence agreement.

# 5. Multi-user Software

Since the introduction of PC LAN and the recognition by software suppliers that MS-DOS V3.x provides a standard for multi-user applications, such applications have begun to appear on the market. In the history of computing this is a strange and unique occurrence because MS-DOS is very definitely a single user operating system and yet there are many multi-user applications that run under it! Of course the reason for this is the use of MS-DOS in a networked environment which is inherently multi-user. It is worth bearing in mind that while this may be obvious to you there are many users and programmers who never give the multi-user aspects of MS-DOS a moment's thought. Indeed there are many who assume that the multi-user aspects of networks are provided in some mysterious way by the network and this has nothing to do with MS-DOS. This has caused a great deal of confusion and many network programs are written specifically for a single proprietary product rather than to a standard that will run on all MS-DOS based networks.

This situation is changing rapidly with the increased awareness that MS-DOS V3.x is the network standard. Even so you still need to exercise care in interpreting which sort of network a piece of software will run on. In this chapter we take a look at multi-user networking standards, some of the packages that run under them and the problems of creating a good multi-user system.

# STANDARDS – MS-DOS V3.x AND NETBIOS

When IBM introduced the PC LAN program they also introduced a standard for multi-user networking software. Although PC LAN is an IBM product it is also available as MS-NET from other manufacturers. Not all existing networks are compatible with this standard as many were designed before IBM introduced its networking product. However nearly all networks that are currently not PC LAN compatible are planning to release new versions of their software to make them so.

To understand a little of what this compatibility entails we need to take a look at two of the components of the PC LAN software. IBM based its network on MS-DOS V3.1 and introduced a new piece of software – the NETBIOS – to allow for variations in network hardware. The role of the NETBIOS to PC LAN is similar to that of the BIOS in relation to MS-DOS. The BIOS (Basic Input Output System) is used by MS-DOS to access all of the PC's hardware. It plays the role of a low level software interface to devices such as disk drives, graphics displays, keyboards, etc. In the same way the NETBIOS (NET Basic Input Output System) plays the role of a low level software interface to the basic networking hardware, the network adapter card. The whole point of the NETBIOS is that it can be rewritten by other network adapter card manufacturers to provide the same interface that network software written for IBM cards expects. This means that once a manufacturer has a written a NETBIOS for their own hardware it can be used in place of the IBM network adapter. In other words if a NETBIOS exists for a network adapter you can run the PC LAN and compatible software on it.

The NETBIOS provides a very low level interface to the network adapter. All it can really do is establish contact between work-stations and send and receive items of data. In other words, it performs the basic communications functions of the network

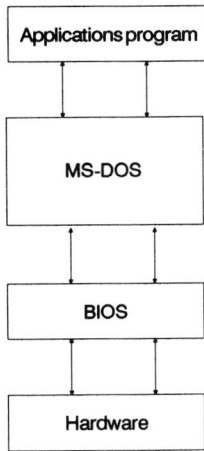

In a non-networked PC applications deal with MS-DOS which deals with the BIOS which finally deals with the hardware

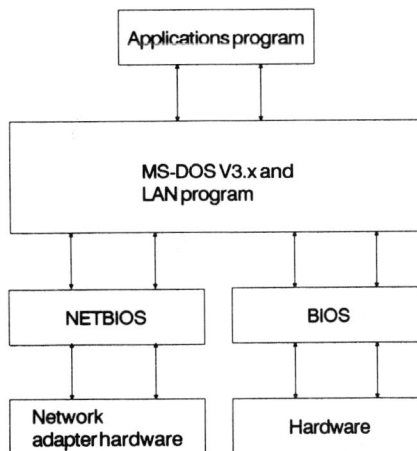

In a networked operating system the NETBIOS deals with the network hardware.

software. If you want to work at the level of files and connections to remote devices you have to move to the level of MS-DOS and PC LAN. Once a connection to a remote device is made all of the file operations needed can be specified by using MS-DOS V3.x. Indeed there are even networking extensions in MS-DOS V3.x that allow a program to make a connection to a device on another machine. In short, although the NETBIOS is in some ways a more fundamental way to access the network, MS-DOS V3.x has nearly everything a program could need and in a form that is more suitable for an application. Despite this many programs do make direct reference to the NETBIOS and this makes them unnecessarily network specific. It is quite possible to implement an MS-DOS V3.x based network without having a NETBIOS.

Thus we can distinguish two levels of network compatibility that a multi-user application program could require:

☐ NETBIOS

☐ MS-DOS V3.x

Some applications programs use mainly MS-DOS V3.x to interact with the network but make the occasional call to the NETBIOS. In future such programs will probably be regarded as 'badly behaved' rather like standard application programs that make use of the BIOS. Although the future looks promising in the sense that MS-DOS V3.x will form a single standard for all networks, at the moment the situation is still confused and it is quite difficult to tell if a network program intended for one network will work on another.

Some network manufacturers offer a NETBIOS module as an optional extra to work with their network adapter. This is often put forward as a guarantee of compatibility. If the software that you want to run doesn't work with their network operating system then you can always buy a NETBIOS. This is not quite the whole story because as well as the NETBIOS you would also have to buy the PC LAN program or an equivalent and this is not a cheap option.

# CONCURRENCY, INTEGRITY AND CONSISTENCY

The aims of a good multi-user program are very simple to state but, as will become clear, very difficult to achieve. A good multi-user program should allow sharing and simultaneous access to data. In other words, it should allow **concurrency** even to qualify as a multi-user program. At the same time as allowing concurrency it should ensure that the data being shared is never damaged by the concurrent accesses. That is, it should ensure the **integrity** of the data at all times. The final mark of a good multi-user program is **consistency**. If possible all users on the network should have the same view of the data even if it is being multiply updated. All multi-user programs have to ensure data integrity but many ignore the problem of consistency. How important this is depends on the nature of the application.

# RECORD AND BYTE RANGE LOCKING

The idea of a resource lock was introduced in the previous chapter as a way of avoiding the problems of simultaneous update of two files by a single user application program. The same idea can be used in multi-user programs to avoid simultaneous update but in this case the lock has to be applied to a smaller unit than a whole file. The reason is simply that a multi-user program has to allow as much sharing of data as possible and should only lock out multiple users from areas of the file that are actually being used. For example, a database generally works in terms of records and as long as no more than one user tries to update any record at a time there are no problems with sharing the file. You should be able to see that this means that records are the resource that have to be locked

User A locks record 502
before making changes
to it.

User B tries to make changes
to record 502

User C locks and
uses record 503

STOP!
Record locked.

Record
502
locked

Record 503 locked

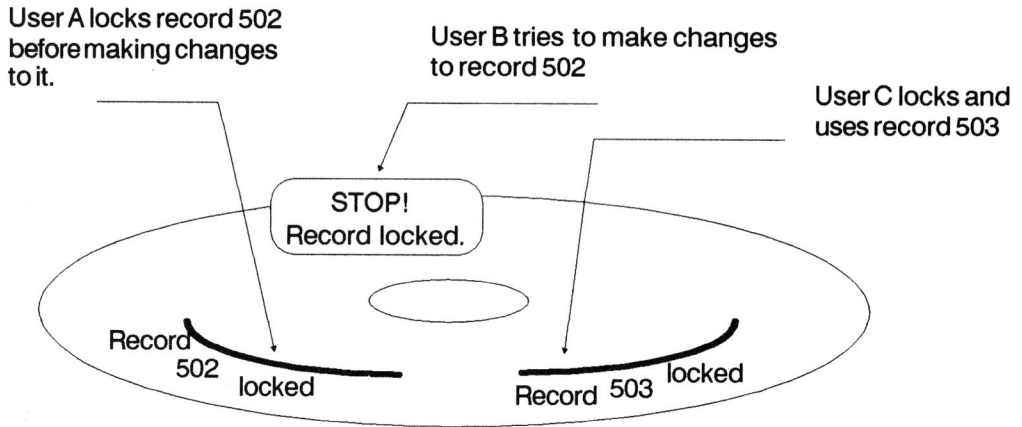

Record locking stops two users changing the same record but user C
can modify a different record within the same file.

rather then entire files – although the true situation is a little more
subtle as we will discover.

Many database programs, dBASE III PLUS for example, provide
default **record locking** and special instruction lock and unlock
commands. If a user wants to edit a particular record then that
record is automatically locked and if another user attempts to edit
the record they will see a message to the effect that the record is in
use and would they like to wait or see another record. In this sense
the record lock is fundamental but in fact there is an even more
fundamental type of lock that lies hidden within the machinery of
MS-DOS V3.x. As well as file locks MS-DOS V3.x provides a **byte
range lock**. This allows a program to lock any portion of a file that
is in use to stop simultaneous access. You should be able to see that
byte range locking is more all embracing than simple record
locking, for example it can be used to implement record locking,
however in most cases record locking is sufficient.

Notice that byte range and hence record locking is provided to the application program entirely by MS-DOS V3.x. Once the network connections between servers and workstations are made, the only network facility that a multi-user database program needs to make use of is record locking and so there should be no need for it to use additional non-MS-DOS calls the NETBIOS or worse completely non-standard calls to the NETWORK software itself. Once again MS-DOS V3.x proves that it is the only networking standard we need.

# SINGLE USER DATABASES ON A NETWORK

Many networks, especially non-MS-DOS V3.x compatible networks, provide explicit commands to allow files and records to be locked. It is possible to use these commands to convert existing single user database programs to multi-user operation. This is only possible if the single user database has a command language that allows database programs to be written and allows calls to external programs or commands. Many existing database programs, for example dBASE II and III, satisfy these conditions and even though they may be available in network versions you may still prefer to stay with your existing single user versions. However implementing a successful database sharing scheme may be more difficult than it appears on first sight.

As long as all the users are simply reading records then there is no need for any sort of file or record locking. As should be clear after the previous chapter, the problems with sharing data only arise when one or more users want to modify the data. If the likelihood of users viewing old data because a record has been updated after they read the information it contains then the only problem is simultaneous update. Clearly this can be solved by locking a record before it is modified and unlocking it after it has been written back to the file. That is the sequence of operations is:

find record
lock record
modify record
write record
unlock record

If the attempt to lock the record fails because the record is already locked then the program should give the user the option of retrying or going on to do something else. This is a simple procedure that seems to guarantee that users cannot update the same record at the same time but it has a dangerous flaw. If the application program uses local buffers (areas of memory) to hold a record then the write record operation may not actually update the disk image of the record. This means that another user could read and update the old version of the record and which change was effective would depend on the order that the buffers were written to disk. The only solution to this problem is to not unlock the record until all of the applications buffers have been written or **flushed** to disk. Some single user programs have an explicit flush command. With others the only option is to close the file and re-open it and this tends to be slow.

Even if you can avoid the buffer problem there are still serious deficiencies with the simple approach outlined above. In particular it takes no account of any index file which may be in use. An index file is a secondary file that defines the order of the main database file. As long as your modifications to the record don't alter the field that it is indexed on there is no need to modify the index file. However how can you know if a modification does alter the index field? In practice the index file has to be locked for every record update. This sounds innocent enough but as this is a file lock and the index file has to be shared by all the updating users this immediately restricts the number of simultaneous updates to one! This isn't much better than using file locks on the entire database file.

# *HIGH CONCURRENCY*

It is relatively easy to implement a multi-user database that is safe – simply apply a file lock every time a modification has to be made. As explained in the previous section this effectively blocks simultaneous update of the database and this isn't really in the spirit of a multi-user application. This highlights the fact that it is not enough to ask if a database is multi-user you also have to ask how multi-user it is. Ideally the sort of multi-user access we would like would allow as many simultaneous users as possible irrespective of what they were doing. In other words the database should apply as few locks for as little time as possible. This is often referred to as a **high concurrency** database. As we have seen it is difficult to implement a high concurrency database using modifications to single user products. What is perhaps more surprising is that many products designed specifically for network use do not achieve high concurrency. They may be multi-user safe but they achieve this by making their users wait while tasks are completed one after another.

A high concurrency multi-user database will only lock a record when it is absolutely necessary and never applies a lock while a user is interacting with the program. For example, if the user wants to modify a record then rather than locking it and possibly the index file for the entire time that the new data is being typed in it should only be locked while the data is being written. That is the sequence of operations should be:

☐ find record display record

☐ get modification into memory variables

☐ lock record

☐ write modifications

☐ unlock record

This avoids the record and index file being locked for the perhaps lengthy interactive data entry. Even in this method there lurks a possible danger. Suppose the interactive data entry goes on for long enough to allow some other user to modify the record – after all the record isn't locked during the data entry? One possible solution to this problem is to lock and re-read the record just before it is written. If the record has been modified by another user since it was first read then this can be detected by the fact that its field values will have changed.

There are many other similar methods that will increase the level of concurrency of a multi-user database. The point is that at the very least a multi-user database should avoid all possibility of data corruption due to simultaneous access but just doing this doesn't make it a good high concurrency multi-user product.

## THE NEED FOR FILE LOCKS

Although for much of the time a simultaneous access can be handled using nothing but record locks, there are times when changes have to be made that affect the entire file. For example, adding records to the end of a file affects its directory entry and in many cases this needs exclusive use of a file. Similarly packing a database to remove deleted entries is a complete reorganisation of the file and again needs exclusive use. Obviously in a high concurrency system such operations should be avoided or at least minimised. Often there are ways to avoid or convert such operations into non-multi-user batch jobs. For example, the need to append records and so lock the entire file can be avoided by keeping a set of dummy records at the end of the file. These can be created each day when the program is first started up and then users can achieve the same effect as appending records without having to lock the file. Of course if an index file is in use modifying a blank record will need the index to be updated so that the new record takes its rightful place in the order of the file but the lock should be in force for a tolerably short time. You could even avoid having to pack the database by converting deleted records to dummy records at the end of the file. If the stock of dummy records is used up then there is still the problem of what to do. You could either accept the worst and lock the file for the duration of the append or you could use a temporary file approach to convert the operation to an off-line batch job. Records could be entered and saved in a private file and then the database program could attempt to add them to the master file at a time when it was OK to lock the database.

For a really high concurrency database it is possible to imagine locking smaller portions of a file than a single record. In particular you could use **field locks** to enable different users to update different fields within the same record! Most database programs don't go that far but many do go to the trouble of only writing the field to the disk image of a record that has actually been altered by the user. In this way it is possible to implement locking schemes that do allow users to modify different fields of the same record. However this sort of thing is for experts only and it is enough to know that it is possible and possibly represents the ultimate in data sharing!

Even if you use as many techniques as possible for avoiding locking the main database file there is still the problem of how to avoid locking any index files that are in use. Adding, deleting or modifying a record usually involves some sort of total reorganisation of the index file and hence a file lock. Generally speaking there are no easy additional techniques that will avoid the need for an index lock. However some database programs use an index organisation (such as a B+ tree) which avoids the need to lock the whole of the index. These are the databases to look at if you really need high concurrency operation.

# DATABASE SERVERS

In many ways our whole approach towards multi-user high concurrency databases as described so far starts from the wrong point. Starting from existing single user databases and simply adding file and record locking is merely a temporary phase needed to convert existing software to network use. It borrows from the methods invented to produce high concurrency databases on multi-user mainframes. A truly networking approach is to consider the role of the disk server in supplying information to the database programs running on the remote workstations. The server knows at all times which records the various stations are asking for and what changes they are making to the index.

The obvious thing to do is to write a different version of the database program to run on the server to the one that runs on the workstations. The workstation database would interact with the server at a much higher level than with a standard operating system and this means that data sharing can be more sophisticated and more efficient. In particular, network traffic can be reduced by the remote workstation sending requests to the server for a particular record and by having the server scan the database rather than pass every record to the workstation for scrutiny. (See the section on database servers in Chapter 3.)

At the moment a number of database manufacturers are promising such database servers. For example, dBASEIV, Emerald Bay and Advanced Revelation all promise either their own database server or support for other manufacturers standard servers. An important standard for the emerging database servers is SQL (Structured Query Language). SQL defines a standard language for accessing databases and, if adopted by enough database manufacturers, should provide a degree of exchangeability between products.

# WHEN THINGS GO WRONG

Any sort of computer failure while a program is running can be devastating, and this is particularly true of a database. The problem of recovering from a failure when the database is being accessed over a network is even more troublesome. In many cases the only solution is to delete the database files and restore them from the most recent backup. Of course this means that users have to be told to re-enter all transactions that took place after the backup was made. To aid in this keeping a log of all transactions is a good idea. Most database programs can be arranged so that a transaction log can be created at each workstation but it is usually up to each user to use this log to recreate the file. Some of the more recent systems now include features such as an automatic transaction log with the ability to un-do or **roll back** any number of transactions to restore the database to an earlier state. Whether this sort of feature is important depends very much on the complexity of your data entry procedures.

# SOME REAL DATABASES

### dBASE III PLUS
Although dBASE II and III have been used successfully in multi-user environments by the addition of special locking routines, dBASE III PLUS was the first version to provide multi-user commands. At the time of writing three networks were supported – PC LAN, 3Com and Novell. Of course the PC LAN support means that it should be possible to run on any MS-DOS V3.x network – specifically Corvus, Mapnet and Zeronet. The standard single user version of dBASE III plus comes with a network version and an installation program that allows one user to access the program over the network. Once installed five additional users can be added for every LAN disk bought.

The range of additional commands include file and record locking. Automatic locking is also supported if the program is used interactively (i.e. from the dot prompt) but this often results in the locking of the entire file. To be of any use you have to convert any single user dBASE programs into multi-user form. The degree of concurrency that you achieve does depend very much on how cleverly this is done. If record and file locks are simply placed at obvious (and safe) points throughout a program then the result is that the file and index file are often required for exclusive use with a resulting slowing down of the operation of the entire system. However with a little care and the sort of techniques described in previous sections, a high concurrency system can be created but it can take a lot of programmer time.

**dBASE IV**
dBASE IV, it is promised, will support networking via an SQL database server. If you are considering a future networking database then it could be very worthwhile examining dBASE IV but at the time of writing very little is known of this successor to the dBASE III standard.

**dBASE clones**
There are many dBASE look-alikes on the market and most of these have followed the dBASE approach to networking. Both Clipper and Foxbase have very similar file and record locking properties to dBASE and the same sort of techniques are necessary to produce a high concurrency system. However it is worth noticing that both of these programs produce dBASE code that runs faster than the real thing and this has to be an advantage when it comes to networking.

A product that is particularly interesting from the networking point of view is dBFast. This is a relatively recent dBASE compiler and its implementers seem to have grasped some of the realities of networking. For example, rather than giving a list of networks they support, they simply say that dBFast will work on any MS-DOS V3.1/NETBIOS 3.1 compatible networks. As well as the standard dBASE networking commands dBFast also introduces two additional commands that are very welcome. The Autolock command enforces an automatic record lock but only when the record is actually written to the disk. It also re-reads the record and ensures that only fields that have actually been modified by the user are altered. This allows a certain amount of simultaneous updating of different fields within the same record. The RLOCKRE command can be used in conjunction with the Autolock command to make sure that simultaneous update of the same field of a record cannot occur. This command locks and then reads the record so that it can be compared with a previous reading stored in a memory variable.

## EMERALD BAY
Emerald Bay is a new database program designed with networking in mind. A very sophisticated database server is promised for the near future which will support SQL and high level languages. The database is highly concurrent and offers advanced features such as transaction logging and roll back.

## ADVANCED REVELATION
The Advanced Revelation database has its origins in the Pick operating system – a multi-user operating system so you would expect it to be well suited to network operation. It uses a special form of index that is particularly well suited to sharing because only portions of it have to be locked during an update. It has an application generator that automatically adds locking statements and it can deal with database files that span more than one device on more than one server – a facility that is currently unique.

## PARADOX VERSION 2
The latest version of Paradox, 2.1, has extensive support for networking that makes it possible to use it interactively while sharing database files. It takes a very intelligent approach to locking

files and records that gives it high concurrency. That is Paradox really does allow many users to work on the same files. There is a special Coedit mode which applies automatic record locking to a file. If the file is indexed then entering a new record or changing the key field of an existing record causes the record to move to its correct position in the file as soon as the change is written (or **posted** in Paradox jargon). There is also a refresh facility that automatically updates a data display at set periods to show changes that other users may have made. This feature makes Paradox particularly useful on a network where data has to reflect the current state of the database. In the same spirit a record is also refreshed if you attempt to lock it or change it. Consistency is ensured when a report is to be generated by taking a snapshot copy of the database before running the report. Thus unlike other database programs reports can be produced without demanding exclusive use of the database files. Of course making a snapshot copy may take time if the database is large and there are a lot of other users but you can always choose to lock the file for exclusive use if speed is important.

The same record locking and refresh capabilities have been added to Paradox's programming language PAL which can be used to implement high concurrency and consistent database programs. All of this makes Paradox one of the few database packages well adapted to network use.

## OPEN ACCESS II

Open Access II is an integrated package – spreadsheet, database, graphics, comms and word-processing – that is available in a network form. It is the first multi-user package that will allow users to share the same the same spreadsheet. This allows more than one user to be looking at and changing the same spreadsheet. Any changes are immediately transmitted across the network to the users looking at the same spreadsheet. In this way all users are kept up to date all of the time. The network version includes an E-mail module.

# MULTI-USER HIGH LEVEL LANGUAGES

Another approach to creating database programs is to use a high level language such as Cobol or BASIC. This approach is tending to go out of favour because of its cost and the availability of off-the-shelf packages. However as far as networking is concerned at the moment the off-the-shelf packages aren't really up to the job and so using a high level language is still a reasonable course of action if you want to get the best out of a network.

There are some high level languages that provide record locking commands and even indexing facilities and clearly these are easier to use to create a multi-user database. However even languages that do not incorporate such refinements can usually be used as long as the appropriate low level calls to the MS-DOS V3.x locking facilities can be made. For example, Turbo BASIC makes it very easy to make MS-DOS calls and so it is suitable for multi-user implementation even though it doesn't have locking commands.

Language implementations that do have locking commands include:

☐ Ryan-McFarland Cobol (network version)

☐ Mallard BASIC (multi-user version)

☐ BASIC2

It is worth mentioning that Mallard BASIC and BASIC2 are both inexpensive and include the same indexed sequential file management system that make implementing databases relatively easy. BASIC2 also has an easy to use GEM interface.

# NETWORK APPLICATION?

As networks become more important and commonplace, the distinction between network software and the applications software that runs under it is becoming blurred. Many specialist networking companies are now producing network software that includes many of the components normally thought of as applications software. This is very reasonable as it is only software designed with networking in mind from the word go that can hope to utilise the network environment to its fullest. Networking is even sufficiently different from a mainframe multi-user environment to need some new thinking and only time will tell what new ways of using networked PCs remains to be invented.

# *SUMMARY*

- ■ MS-DOS V3.x and NETBIOS are the two most important standards for multi-user applications software.

- ■ A good multi-user program would ensure high concurrency, data integrity and consistency at all times.

- ■ Record locking is used to allow database files to be shared.

- ■ MS-DOS V3.x provides byte range locking which can be used to implement record locking and other more sophisticated schemes.

- ■ Achieving high concurrency using a simple minded approach to record locking is very difficult.

- ■ Even though it may appear that only a record lock is needed, very often an operation will require a file lock to be placed on a shared index. This can reduce the amount of concurrency possible to unacceptable levels.

- ■ In the future database servers will replace simple file servers and so reduce network traffic for operations that require a scan of the entire database file.

- ■ Additional features such as backup and error recovery can also determine which database program suits your network application best.

# 6. Some Real Products

Although most of the central ideas of networking have been described and discussed in previous chapters it is important to examine some real networks to see how these ideas work in practice. Of course the difficulty is which networks to look at. In the world of computing, products come onto the market very rapidly and as a result any market survey dates equally quickly. Fortunately in networking it is possible to identify well established examples of each type of network. Other products that appear in the future must be more or less like one of these types. So while this chapter doesn't set out to be a market survey, it should help you to evaluate any network that you may meet now or in the future. Most applications software and hardware mentions at least three networks – PC LAN, 3Com and Novell Netware – in their configuration instructions, and these three are generally regarded as the most common standards.

It is difficult to state a set of criteria by which network software can be measured. What matters most depends very much on the main purpose to which the network is put:

☐ Good easy to use and efficient file sharing is clearly important.

☐ A network should either allow drives to be shared at the directory level or should allow the SUBST or a network equivalent to be used to assign a drive's identifier to directories.

☐ The sort of naming a network uses can alter the way it looks to the user.

☐ The importance of security varies from application to application.

☐ The level of E-mail needed depends on the size and nature of the organisation that the network will serve.

Bearing these points in mind, the descriptions of the networks given below should serve to give you some idea of what to expect from your proposed network.

## IBM's LAN

Although IBM's main PC network offering cannot be considered amongst the cheapest, it has set the software standard for most other networks. For this reason it is important to know something about it, if only to decide how well the other networks mimic it. There are two clear components to the PC LAN – the network hardware and the network software. From the point of view of other networks it is only the network software that is important as this can be made to run on almost any hardware. Indeed IBM offer two types of network hardware that the PC LAN software can be run on.

## HARDWARE – PC NETWORK

The PC Network is a bus network but it is unusual in being a broadband system. A **broadband** network converts the digital pulses that form the fundamental method of communications between computers to a radio frequency signal similar to that used by a television station. The main advantage of this technique is that the signal can share a cable with other forms of communication in much the same way that an aerial cable can carry the signal from a great many radio and TV stations. A broadband network can thus save cabling costs either by using existing cables or allowing cables to be shared. The characteristics of the PC Network are:

| | |
|---|---|
| Topology | Bus |
| Cabling | Coaxial (like Cheapernet) |
| Speed | 2Mbps |
| Max. workstations | 72 |
| Max. distance | 300m |
| Notes | Broadband system capable of sharing cabling with other signals such as TV, radio and voice. |

Apart from being a broadband system the PC LAN is very much like other medium to high speed PC networks.

# TOKEN RING

The second type of network hardware that IBM offer is more unusual in being a token ring. In a token ring network a group of PCs are connected by a ring of cable and messages are passed from PC to PC around this ring. The advantages of a token ring are that a greater distance can be covered and the design even allows for separate rings to be connected together to form very large networks. One interesting point about the IBM token ring is that while the connection pattern is indeed a ring this is formed by connecting each machine to a central access unit. This means that the actual wiring pattern is a star rather than a ring. The characteristics of the IBM token ring network are:

| | |
|---|---|
| Topology | Ring but cabled as a star |
| Cabling | Coaxial, twisted pair or fibre optic |
| Speed | 4Mbps (100Mbps on fibre optics) |

| | |
|---|---|
| Max. workstations | 72 on twisted pair, 260 on coaxial but multiple rings can be linked together almost without limit |
| Max. distance | Virtually unlimited |
| Notes | Mainly used for large installations |

# SOFTWARE – PC LAN (MS-NET)

As already mentioned, IBM's contribution to networking goes beyond the two types of hardware described above because of the standards established by the PC LAN software. The PC LAN program is also available from other manufacturers as MS-NET. The relationship of PC LAN to MS-NET is very much like the relationship of PC-DOS and MS-DOS. PC-DOS is IBM's version of MS-DOS in the same way that PC LAN is IBM's version of MS-NET. There may be minor differences in the utilities and other additional software between PC LAN and MS-NET but they are essentially the same. From this point on all descriptions of the PC LAN should be taken as referring to MS-NET as well. Any differences will be explicitly mentioned.

The key features of PC LAN are:

☐ Four types of workstation configuration server, messenger, receiver and redirector.

☐ Disk sharing at the directory level. That is, directories are shared as well as whole devices.

☐ A network-wide naming system for workstations and shared devices.

☐ A simple message passing system, including message logging to disk and forwarding.

Every workstation on the network has to have a network name. This is determined using the NET START name command which logs the workstation on to the network under and calls it name.

Each workstation on the network can be also be configured to one of the four types using the NET START command (usually in the autoexec.bat file). The types of workstation form a hierarchy of increasing network capabilities. The simplest workstation is a redirector. This can use network devices and send messages but not receive them. A receiver can do everything that a redirector can, but it can receive and save messages as well. A messenger can do everything a receiver can as well as adding user names and receiving forwarded messages. Finally a full server can do all of the previous network functions as well as offering its local devices for use by other workstations.

The only real advantage of configuring a PC for minimum network function is to save memory. In most cases the only worthwhile distinction to be made is server/non-server. This means that most PC LAN workstations consist of only servers and messengers.

A server can offer any of its devices for sharing by the other workstations. For example, to offer an entire hard disk for use by the rest of the network you would type

NET SHARE APP=C:\

which allows other workstations to share the root directory of your C: drive, giving it the network name APP. Following this command another user can connect to C:\ by using the command

NET USE D: \\MASTER\APP

where the server stations name is MASTER. The notation

\\workstation_name\share_name

was introduced with the PC LAN and it has been adopted by a

number of other networks that allow naming of workstations and resources.

Following this command the local disk drive D: is taken to refer to the remote drive C: on MASTER. If you want to you can use a remote drive without assigning a local disk drive letter to it but then you have to refer to the remote drive by its full name. For example, after

NET USE \\MASTER\APP

the disk has to be referred to as \\MASTER\APP.

Notice that the method of sharing resources involves the server station assigning a name – a **share name** or a **network name** – to the device using the NET SHARE command, which can then be used by a workstation to connect to the resource by way of the NET USE command.

The general form of the NET SHARE command is

NET SHARE network_name=resource_name password permission

where network_name is the name that remote stations use to refer to the resource, resource_name is the local name of the resource, password is an optional password that the user has to supply to connect to the resource and permission is the type of access that is allowed. This can be any of or any combination of:

/R – read
/W – write
/C – create

If you don't specify a permission then /RWC is assumed. The resource name can be a path name on a disk drive to make a directory shareable or it can be a device name such as LPT1 to share a standard MS-DOS device. For example,

NET SHARE accounts=C:\apps\sc\data ABC /R

makes the directory C:\apps\sc\data shareable as accounts for reading only, with the user having to know the password ABC

NET SHARE laser1=LPT1

makes the printer connected to printer port 1 shareable as laser1.

The general form of the NET USE command is

NET USE local_device \\server_name\network_name password

where local_device is an optional local device that will be connected to the remote resource, \\server_name is the name of the workstation that is providing the resource, network_name is the name given to the device by the server and password is the optional password set by the server. For example, to connect drive E: to accounts (as defined above) you would use

NET USE E: \\master1\accounts ABC

assuming that the sever name is called master1. To connect LPT1 to the remote printer laser you would use

NET USE LPT1 \\master1\laser

Output sent to a shared printer is automatically spooled at the server but there is a NET PRINT command to send files of output to the printer which works in much the same way as the standard MS-DOS PRINT command.

To find out what devices a server has offered to share simply type

NET SHARE

which produces a list of shared devices. Similarly

NET USE

will produce a list of connected devices.

The PC LAN messaging service is very basic but functional. You can send short messages to any workstation simply by using the NET SEND command. For example

NET SEND tom How about lunch

sends the message "How about lunch" to the workstation named tom. You can send a message to everyone using the name ★ as in

NET SEND ★ About to shut the system down

You can divert messages to a file so that they don't disturb you using the NET LOG command. You can also receive messages for other users by use of the NET NAME command. For example, following the command

NET NAME tom

---

### TABLE 1   PC LAN commands

| NET | Start the network using a menu |
|---|---|
| NET START name type | Start using the network as name and type |
| NET SEND | Send a message |
| NET LOG | Save incoming messages in a log |
| NET NAME name | Receive messages for name |
| NET FORWARD | Forward messages |
| NET SHARE | Permit remote access to a resource |
| PERMIT | Permit exclusive access to a resource |
| NET SEPARATOR | Insert a separator page between spooled documents |
| NET FILE | List files, current users and locks |
| NET USE | Use a shared resource |
| NET PRINT | Network version of MS-DOS PRINT |
| NET PAUSE | Temporary pause of network use |
| NET CONTINUE | Restart after a pause |
| NET ERROR | List errors |

---

your workstation will receive messages for tom even though it isn't called tom. In the same way you can arrange for your messages to be forwarded to another station using the NET FORWARD name1 name2 which forwards messages sent to name1 to name2. This is clearly not an E-mail facility but it is sometimes handy.

As well as controlling the network by entering commands, the user can also enter a menu driven system by simply typing NET. This is sometimes easier to use but in general most of the network commands needed to configure a network would be included in a batch file. A list of PC LAN commands can be seen in Table 1.

IBM have recently announced PC LAN V1.3 which adds a number of enhancements. In particular the network manager can now remotely control a server, users can be assigned passwords for logon, remote initial program load and remote workstation print queue access and control.

# APRICOT NETWORKS – MS-NET

MS-NET is broadly like PC LAN but with different manufacturer's customisations and of course network hardware. Although MS-NET is a Microsoft product they do not support it directly and direct potential and current users to the suppliers of network hardware and machines. Apricot Computers are one of the leading suppliers of MS-NET based systems and their implementation of MS-NET has a number of improvements over PC LAN. The main hardware that they offer is Omninet, which is a 1Mbps bus network (see Corvus) but this is largely irrelevant as the same version of MS-NET will run on a range of networking hardware. The main enhancements made to the raw MS-NET are:

☐ The addition of a remote boot server to support diskless workstations.

☐ A time server which supplies a standard synchronised time for all workstations.

☐ A console manager that allows dedicated file servers without keyboard or screen to be controlled from another workstation.

☐ File servers can work with disks larger than the 32M MS-DOS limit.

☐ Improved printer spooling facilities.

All-in-all the Apricot version of MS-NET is a much more usable product which includes copious high quality documentation, management and diagnostic aids and advice. They are also one of the few networking specialists who consider how the network should be used in applications and their documentation doesn't stop at the basic setting up of the network but suggests ways of managing the network.

## CORVUS – THE AMSTRAD NETWORK

Corvus have been supplying low cost networks for some time and many of their products pre-date the introduction of the PC LAN standards. However their latest network operating system PC/NOS is MS-DOS V3.x compatible which means that it should be possible to run any software that works on the PC LAN (or MS-NET) under PC/NOS. There is also an optional NETBIOS which can be run along with PC/NOS to provide for applications programs that need to access the network card at a lower level. Corvus have a well developed range of networking products which span the full range of applications.

As well as serving the higher cost networking market Corvus also have a low cost network, Omninet/1, which is compatible with the rest of their range. Omninet/1 is very cost effective and it has been selected by Amstrad to be 'badged' as their own network. In its

Amstrad version it is little changed from the Corvus branded version. There are a few improvements to the user interface and the installation instructions but even these will be incorporated into the Corvus product in time.

# HARDWARE – OMNINET/1 AND OMNINET/4

Corvus produce two bus networks, Omninet/1 which runs at 1Mbps and Omninet/4 which runs at 4Mbps. Both use a twisted pair cabling system and there is a simple to use snap together cabling kit. The original Omninet cabling system allowed active T-junctions so that cable could be laid in a tree pattern but even so the basic network is still a bus. The older cabling system used junction boxes with a mixture of phone style and miniature jack plugs. The new cabling system is composed of junction boxes which have sockets not only for the workstation's spur cable but for the incoming and outgoing trunk cable. In principle you can 'snap' together a wiring scheme in a few minutes without using even a screwdriver. There is also an optical fibre link that can link two LAN segments up to 2Km apart. The characteristics of the Omninet hardware are:

| | |
|---|---|
| Topology | Bus |
| Cabling | Twisted pair |
| Speed | 1Mbps (Omninet/1) 4Mbps (Omninet/4) |
| Max. workstations | 64 |
| Max. distance | 300m (1.2Km using repeaters ever 300m) |
| Notes | Easy to use cabling system. |

As well as basic network hardware Corvus also produce a range of ancillary hardware. In particular they have a 386 and a 286 based file server, a range of dedicated file servers (Omnidrive) and a dedicated printer server. They also have a range of gateway hardware and software that enables an Omninet system to link to mainframes – specifically, SNA/3270, X25 and DEC.

It is also worth mentioning that at the time of writing the basic Omninet/1 network adapter card is one of the lowest cost available (£99). However this price doesn't include software which has to be taken into account at £595 for an unlimited number of users.

## SOFTWARE

Both Corvus networks use the PC/NOS program. This is an MS-DOS V3.x compatible network operating system. You can run it with earlier versions of MS-DOS if you must, but this prohibits from making use of locking. There is also an optional NETBIOS that can be loaded at the same time as PC/NOS to ensure full PC LAN compatibility. The Corvus networks are often left out of network installation procedures for applications software but in general you should install as if the network was PC LAN. If the software fails to run then you need to install the NETBIOS as well as PC/NOS.

The main characteristics of a PC/NOS network are:

☐ Three types of workstation – full server, small server and client.

☐ Fixed node and user names with the ability to share devices or directories.

☐ The use of disk caching to speed server operations.

☐ Menu driven user interface.

The only difference between the full and small server workstations is efficiency and memory usage. A full server uses an additional memory of 300K or larger to make file service fast. A small server uses roughly half the amount of memory and this makes it more feasible to run applications software while sharing disks. The full server can be used as a workstation if the application fits in the remaining memory, and you can even use extended memory boards to go beyond the 640K limit. In practice however you should think seriously about dedicating full servers to the task that they have been optimised for. PC/NOS in workstations only takes 71K of extra memory, and stations with this installed can use shared resources but cannot offer any of their own local resources to the network.

The resources in PC/NOS are managed by being regarded as belonging to various modules. The terminology for an available shared resource is a 'socket' and local device names that can be connected to a socket are called 'plug's. Each socket and plug belongs to a particular type of PC/NOS module that is responsible for providing one class of service. For example, all disk and file resources (plugs and sockets) are provided by the MS-DOS module, and all printer spooling resources are provided by the spooler module.

A user can make a connection between any plug and any socket, so giving access to a remote resource. For example, if a disk server offers a hard disk as a socket C: then a user can connect a plug D: to it and from that point on any reference to D: will use the remote drive C:. Each workstation has a fixed name and so does each user of the network. PC/NOS allows the network manager to set up resource and user profiles that control access to the network. Connections can be made in two ways: automatically as users log on, or the user can connect to the services that are on offer manually. Most network connections and resource file modifications would be made using the menu driven NETVIEW program but there are command line equivalents for most menu options. For example, if a user at node STAT2 wants to connect drive E: to drive C: on node SERV1 they could use the command

NV CON STAT2/MS-DOS/E: = SERV21/msdos/C:

The general form of a connection command is

NV CON plug_node_name/module/plug=socket_node_name/
module/socket

Unlike PC LAN/MS-NET there is no use of share or network names that can be used by workstations to refer to shared resources. However the use of node, or workstation names, and the fact that connections can be made by selecting shared resources from a menu in NETVIEW, make PC/NOS easy to use. The need to make use of, or even know about, module names seems to be an unnecessary complication from the user's point of view.

A server can provide printer spooling, remote booting for diskless workstations and share its COM ports or any other MS-DOS devices directly. One shortcoming of PC/NOS is its inability to share disk drives larger than the 32Mb MS-DOS limit without dividing them up into partitions smaller than 32Mb. A limited time service is also provided by allowing a workstation to connect to the server's clock, read and set the local clock and then disconnect. Security is enforced by logon passwords and users can be assigned privilege levels and belong to one of four user groups. Each device can be assigned a security level and a user must have at least as high a privilege level to be allowed to use the device. This is a good method of controlling access to the network and allows users to be 'zoned' into various levels of privilege.

The message passing facilities of PC/NOS are fairly limited but Corvus do sell an add on E-mail system. Any user can send a short (less than 1000 characters) message to another user. If the user is not connected then a deferred message can be sent which will only be delivered when the user logs on.

As well as the basic PC/NOS software Corvus can supply and support a wide range of extras. CC:Mail is an electronic mail system that can send messages that consist of any sort of MS-DOS file from one workstation to another. NOSTalk is a network communications package that allows a number of users to share the same modem. Of course simultaneous sharing is impossible because of the nature of a modem but users can join a queue to use the modem and be informed when it is free. As well as the gateways to connect the Omninet system to mainframe computers Corvus also offer a Constellation to PC/NOS connection. This enables a mixed network of Apple MACs, Apple IIs and PCs to be set-up. This allows the file transfer between both types of machine and the PCs can use the Apple laser writer. Finally if in the unlikely event that you find that PC/NOS not up to the job you can always buy Novell's Netware for the Omninet network adapters.

## 3Com

3Com, like Corvus, have been in the network business for a long time. Their latest product 3Share is an MS-DOS V3.x/NETBIOS compatible network. In other words, it should be possible to run any applications programs that will run under PC LAN or MS-NET. They also manufacture a wide range of hardware and software products to enable a simple network to grow into a large complex network. They offer a diskless 80286 workstation complete with a built in Ethernet interface, a number of high capacity disk and printer servers and an SNA interface to IBM mainframes.

## HARDWARE

The 3Com network hardware is based on a standard Ethernet system and a standard PC Token ring system. As both of these are standard networks there is very little to say about them! The Ethernet system can use standard Ethernet cable or Cheapernet. There is also a special wiring module that allows two cores of a standard telephone cable to be used in an Ethernet system. The specification of the Ethernet system is:

| | |
|---|---|
| Topology | Bus |
| Cabling | Ethernet or Cheapernet |
| Speed | 10Mbps |
| Max. workstations | 100 Ethernet (30 Cheapernet) |
| Max. distance | 500m Ethernet (300m Cheapernet) |
| | 1000m using repeaters (990m Cheapernet) |
| Notes | A special cable driver is available for using twisted pair cables over short distances. |

The token ring hardware is standard apart from the choice of cabling systems. You can use the IBM Cabling System for complete compatibility or you can use 3Com's own RingTap and Token Plus cabling system for convenience. This allows a Token ring to be wired as a bus system. The details of 3Com's token ring hardware are:

| | |
|---|---|
| Topology | Ring but cabled as a star (IBM) or a bus (3COM) |
| Cabling | Coaxial, twisted pair or fibre optic |
| Speed | 4Mbps (100mbps on fibre optics) |
| Max. workstations | 72 on twisted pair, 260 on coaxial, 250 on 3Com's cabling system but multiple rings can be linked together almost without limit |
| Max. distance | Virtually unlimited |
| Notes | Mainly used for large installations. |

# SOFTWARE

3Com's networking software is extensive but its main or core product is 3+Share. This is an MS-DOS V3.x and NETBIOS compatible network operating system. It is composed of three separate pieces of software:

☐ 3+File/Print   which looks after disk and printer sharing

☐ 3+Name        which provides a centralised name service

☐ 3+Menu        an easy-to-use WIMP interface

The 3+Share operating system is very similar to an enhanced version of the PC LAN program in its approach towards naming, sharing of resources and commands. The main characteristics of 3Com's network software are:

☐ Disk sharing at the directory level.

☐ High efficiency filing system.

☐ Centralised name service for workstations and resources.

☐ Extended naming system allows inter-network communication.

☐ Aliases allow short names to be used.

The 3+Share network software allows the creation of names for workstations, directories and access rights. The naming of resources follows the IBM convention of

\\workstation_name\share_name.

For example, \\MASTER\LASER refers to the resource called LASER on a server called MASTER. All users and servers are allocated three part names:

name:domain:organisation

where name is the users name, domain is usually the geographical location or department and organisation is the company name. This three part naming can be used to divide up and organise a network. Within a single domain it is only necessary to use the simple name. Adding users' names and servers' names is a job that the network manager is assumed to perform so as to present a uniform and organised view of the network to all users.

Each user is associated with a login file that gives the password, default file server, default mail server etc. Each user has to log in to use the network when their login file is consulted for their configuration. A shared disk on a server has a well defined directory structure. Any direct user of the server is allocated to the directory 3ROOT which appears to be a 'dummy' drive C:. Shared applications are stored in APPS and each user has a personal or home directory that cannot be shared. If a directory is shared then all directories below the one explicitly shared are also shared. To allow some directories to be private 3+Share only allows directories below the root to be shared.

To offer a device for sharing you would use the 3F SHARE command. For example:

3F SHARE ADAT=C:\acc\data /PASS ABC /RWC

which assigns the share name ADAT to the directory C:\acc\data with a password of ABC which makes it available for read, write and create operations. You can also use the

3F SHARE ?

command which then prompts for the name, password, directory to be shared, and the access rights. The access rights can be any combination of read, write and create.

Following this a user can enter the 3F link command to connect a local device name to the shared resource. For example, if a directory \data\account on a server called master has been given the share name acc1 a user can connect drive D: to it using

3F LINK D: \\master\a1

If a password has been set then the system will prompt the user to supply it before making the connection. If you don't mention the name of the server then the default server is assumed. For example, if master is the default server then

3F link D: \acc1

would connect D: to the resource acc1 on the server master.

3+Share supports a fairly standard printer spooling server. Users can alter the priority of files in the print queue. To signal that output from applications programs have finished you have to press CTRL/ALT/PrtSc.

You can see a list of 3+Share commands in Table 2. This list isn't complete because some of the commands that would be used exclusively by the network manager, E-mail commands and archive commands have been omitted. 3+Share commands are grouped into 3F – file commands, 3N – name commands and 3P – printer commands. A user can give any of the commands either by typing the whole instruction or by typing 3F, 3N or 3P to load the appropriate module and then giving just the second word of the command. That is you can type

C>3F SHARE

or

C>3F
3F>SHARE

The advantage of the second method is that you can give as many 3F commands as you require before returning to MS-DOS by entering a blank line.

As well as the command interface, users can also opt to interact with the system by way of the 3+menu service. This allows users to make connections, share resources, send E-mail and run applications programs all by selecting from menus. Additional software modules extend the basic network operating system to include features such as fault tolerance, automatic archiving and E-mail. Fault tolerance is achieved either by using two hard disk drives in

### TABLE 2   3+Share Commands

| | |
|---|---|
| LOGIN | start using the network |
| LOGOUT | stop using the network |
| 3F DIR | display information about shared directories |
| 3F HELP | help information on 3F commands |
| 3F LINK | connect to a shared resource |
| 3F MOD | change password and access rights |
| 3F SHARE | assign a share name and access rights to a resource |
| 3F SHUTDOWN | shut down a specified server |
| 3F STATUS | display status of disks on a server |
| 3F UNLINK | disconnect from a remote device |
| 3F UNSHARE | remove a share name |
| 3N ADD SERVER | add a server name |
| 3N ADD USER | add a user name |
| 3N ASSIGN | give IBM style name to a 3+ three part name |
| 3N DIR | display network names |
| 3N HELP | help information on 3N commands |
| 3N MOD | change login password |
| 3N SET | change of default server, domain or organisation |
| 3N STATUS | information about user name |
| 3P DEL | remove file from spool queue |
| 3P DIR | list shared printers |
| 3P HELP | help information on 3P commands |
| 3P LINK | link printer to printer server |
| 3P QSTAT | status of printer spooling queue |
| 3P SET | set special printing options |
| 3P STATUS | display printer server information |
| 3P UNLINK | disconnect from printer server |

each server to mirror operations or by using two completely identical servers. If a fault develops on one of the disk drives or servers then its dual takes over without users knowing anything about it. There are internetworking products allowing 3+Share to connect with MACs on an Appletalk network, networks linked by modems, IBM mainframes, etc.

# NOVELL

Novell have been producing networking software since well before the introduction of IBM's PC LAN. They have built up a reputation for fast and reliable software but their products are generally not thought of as cheap. However they do offer a four-user entry-level product that is reasonably competitive with products at the lower end of the market. Novell do produce network hardware and their networking software is available for a wide range of other manufacturers hardware. Indeed any manufacturer of networking hardware usually feels obliged to offer the capability to run Novell's software to demonstrate how standard their hardware is. Novell's netware is both MS-DOS and NETBIOS compatible.

# HARDWARE

Novell's software is available for most network hardware but they do produce one of the standard Ethernet cards, the NE1000. This can drive both full Ethernet and Cheapernet systems and it is compatible with many other manufacturers cards. The basic characteristics are:

| | |
|---|---|
| Topology | Bus |
| Cabling | Ethernet or Cheapernet |
| Speed | 10Mbps |
| Max. workstations | 100 Ethernet (30 Cheapernet) |
| Max. distance | 500m Ethernet (300m Cheapernet) |
| | 1000m using repeaters (990m Cheapernet) |

# SOFTWARE

Novell's netware started from a slightly different position to most of the network software described in this chapter. Instead of adding on to MS-DOS or some other multi-user/tasking operating system Novell created an operating system especially for networking. This gave them the chance to design an efficient network operating system but it also raised the possibility of not being compatible with MS-DOS. Practically speaking the biggest difference between Netware and MS-DOS is that it uses a special disk format and filing system. This is optimised for speed and reliability on a network file server.

From a workstation the server's file structure looks like MS-DOS and applications programs can use it as if it was MS-DOS but you cannot remove the networking software and boot an alternative operating system from the same disk. In this sense once a machine is set up as a Novell file server it is quite difficult to change its role. It also means that you cannot directly make use of any of the file management utilities that have appeared for MS-DOS devices. Also prohibited is adding any non-standard MS-DOS devices because the Novell netware device drivers are different. (Netware by-passes the standard ROM BIOS and addresses devices directly for increased network efficiency.)

The basic features of the Novell netware software are:

☐ Disk sharing at the directory level.

☐ Server disks are given volume names.

☐ User and resource names

☐ User profiles for connection and to determine privileges.

☐ A high level of error detection and recovery.

☐ Extensive security facilities.

The new version of Netware V2.1 provides for non-dedicated servers by allowing MS-DOS to be run as a task under Netware. This wasn't true of older versions and it is often a criticism levelled at Netware that a dedicated server is required. One thing that hasn't changed is that Netware is copy protected and needs a key card to run. The entry level version of Netware isn't copy protected but it is limited to four users. (At the time of writing Novell are about to announce an eight-user product.)

Each server is assigned a server name and each disk drive on the server is assigned a volume name. It is possible to divide a disk drive up into a number of volumes but this isn't usual. Every server must have one volume called SYS. To refer to a particular sub-directory on a particular server you have to give the server name, the volume name and the path name of the directory. For example,

FS1/SYS:ACCOUNTS/DATA

refers to the directory ACCOUNTS/DATA on the SYS volume of the server called FS1. Notice how the volume name plays the role of an MS-DOS device name. As file servers have to run special software and use a different format for their hard disks there is no way that a user can offer a hard disk for sharing on a temporary basis. That is all services, volumes, printer spooler etc. are set up when the server software is installed.

Before a workstation can make use of the facilities of a server it has to logon to that server using the LOGIN command which also specifies the user name and password. Each server can be protected with a different password for that user. A successful login results in a script (batch file) being run which configures the user's environment by making connections to the server. A user can explicitly connect to a volume using the MAP command. For example, following

MAP D:=FS1/SYS:/SALES/DATA

### TABLE 3   Novell Netware Commands

| | |
|---|---|
| ATTACH | log on to additional servers |
| CASTOFF | prevent workstation from receiving messages |
| CASTON | allow messages |
| CHKVOL | network equivalent of CHKDSK |
| ENDSPOOL | close a spool file |
| FLAG | network and extended version of ATTR |
| HELP | help information |
| LISTDIR | view directory structure of a volume |
| LOGIN | use a particular server |
| LOGOUT | release server |
| MAP | connect to server directories |
| NCOPY | extended version of copy |
| NPRINT | send a file to the spool queue |
| NSNIPES | a network game |
| PURGE | remove files marked for deletion |
| Q | list and delete spool files |
| RIGHTS | show access permissions in a given directory |
| SALVAGE | recover files marked for deletion |
| SEND | send a short message |
| SETPASS | change password |
| SLIST | view list of available file servers |
| SPOOL | spool output from an application |
| SYSTIME | view a server's system clock and date |
| UDIR | search all sub directories for a file |
| USERLIST | list all logged on users |
| VOLINFO | show the status of server volumes |
| WHOAMI | show user's identity and other details |

any use of drive D: would be taken as a reference to the /SALES/ DATA directory on the SYS volume of the server called SYS. If a user wants to connect to volumes on a server that they are not logged on to they can use the ATTACH command. The only difference between LOGIN and ATTACH is that it doesn't result in a script file being run.

Another interesting detail that results from Netware file servers using a different filing system is that the MS-DOS erase command doesn't really remove the file from the volume, it just marks it for deletion. Files marked for deletion can be recovered but eventually the user or the system manager can physically remove them from the disk using the PURGE command.

A list of the main netware command can be seen in Table 3. Notice that as well as these commands there are also a full range of menu equivalents.

A unique feature of Netware is its accounting facilities. These can be used to charge for network use. Charges can be made for connection time, bytes read or written to disk, storage space or for the number of requests made by the workstation. Rates can vary by the hour or by the day. User's credit limits can be set and users with overdrawn accounts are logged off. This facility can obviously be use to establish a public network in schools, or the PC equivalent of time sharing bureaux.

Novell netware is generally regarded as one of the most efficient network operating systems. It also has a very well developed fault tolerant nature. This can be further extended by using System Fault Tolerant (SFT) Netware on a special Novell 68B file server. (Novell also offer a 286 and 386 file servers.) There is also an archive module, E-mail module and a range of communications modules.

Netware often appears too expensive for a first time or small network situation. However it is wise to choose networking hardware that can run Netware because this offers the opportunity to upgrade if and when the network proves its value and outgrows its original software.

# MAPNET

MAPNET is one of the networks being supplied by an existing business software specialist in an effort to extend their products into a multi-user environment. MAPNET is a complete package of hardware and software and it is of special interest to anyone already using Map software. The network software is MS-DOS V3.x compatible and offers all of the facilities that you would expect of a full network. A NETBIOS module is also available to ensure full PC LAN compatibility. MAPNET is unusual because it defines workstations and servers by hardware and software differences and disk sharing happens automatically as workstations log on to the network. In other words there are no explicit resource sharing commands.

# HARDWARE

The MAPNET adapter cards are unusual in that a different card is used for the server workstation. In other words the identity of the server is determined by which machine has the master board. The cabling system is based on the use of 9-pin D connectors and multi-core cable. Suitable cables are provided with the MAPNET system but the manual also contains instructions on how to make up your own. The system is also unusual in that the speed of transmission can be modified according to the length of the cable. This means you can have a large network that runs slowly or a small network that runs quickly. Installation is simple and very quick and you should be able to get a small network up and running in no time. The hardware characteristics of MAPNET are:

| | |
|---|---|
| Topology | Bus |
| Cabling | Multi-core and 9-pin D connectors |
| Speed | 1.9Mbps down to 0.2Mbps depending on distance |

| Max. workstations | 64 |
|---|---|
| Max. distance | 150m (highest speed) |
| | 1000m (lowest speed) |
| Notes | Workstations can run at different speeds depending on their separation. |

# SOFTWARE

The MAPNET network software is command rather than menu driven. These appear as an additional set of commands to MS-DOS, each one prefaced by the ~ character. The main features of the MAPNET software are:

☐ Resource sharing at the disk drive level.

☐ Automatic connection to the server.

☐ User names, passwords and restricted access to directories for security.

The software that is installed on the master workstation, the disk server, is different from that installed on the rest of the workstations. This automatically determines the way resources are shared across the network. That is the master offers its drive C: (and any other drives above this) for sharing and the workstations automatically connect their first free drive letter to the server. For example, if the server has a single hard disk C: and a workstation has two floppy disks A: and B: its drive C: will be connected to the server's drive C:. You can change these automatic allocations to a certain extent by changing the config.sys files on the workstations but there are no commands that allow users to make connections while the network is running. Although sharing is at the disk drive level there is a special network version of the ~SUBST command which can be used to allocate drive letters to particular directories.

The master station can also offer printer spooling to the rest of the network. There are two ways that a workstation can send output to the server. Following a ~SPOOL command all printer output is saved in a specified disk file until an ~UNSPOOL command is given. Following this the spooled file can be sent to the printer queue with the ~PRINT command. This manual method gets around the problem of defining when one print job is complete and another begins.

The second method of printer spooling attempts to automate the ~SPOOL, ~UNSPOOL and ~PRINT sequence. This uses either a 'hot key' press (Ctrl/right shift, both shift keys or ALT and right shift key) to mark the end of the spool file or a time or size criterion. The most usual way of using this would be to set a reasonable time out so that if the application stopped printing for more than 5 seconds it would be assumed that it had finished printing and the spool file would be closed and added to the queue. This is the method that most of the other networks use to control printer spooling. A more unusual feature is the ability to specify the type of form that a spooled file needs to be printed. The file will wait in the queue until the user of the printer server uses a command to let the server know that the correct form is now in the printer.

Another unusual feature of MAPNET is that there are a great many ways in which its operation can be fine tuned by the network manager. For example, you can set the amount of time that the server spends looking after the network and how long it spends running its own applications software. This is useful because it gives you the choice of how to optimise your network. An optional security system can be installed allowing the system manager to restrict access to directories and give read only, write or erase permissions. The MAPNET commands are can be seen in Table 4.

The biggest advantage of the MAPNET network is that MAP have made sure that its supports its own multi-user software, namely

---

## *Table 4   MAPNET commands*

| | |
|---|---|
| ~~~ | system status |
| ~boot | reboot station |
| ~bye | log off network |
| ~cache | install disk cache |
| ~cancel | remove file from printer queue |
| ~dir | network dir command |
| ~dump | dump memory to provide diagnostic info |
| ~exec | allow workstation to run a program on the master |
| ~files | display open files and lock status |
| ~flag | lock a resource |
| ~form | tell the server what form is loaded in the printer |
| ~free | network equivalent of chkdsk |
| ~help | help |
| ~hi | logon |
| ~hog | occupy memory for testing purposes |
| ~hold | hold a file in the print queue |
| ~licks | allocate processor time to the network/server program |
| ~maptest | test the network |
| ~msg | send a message to a station number |
| ~print | send a file for spooling |
| ~printer | printer status |
| ~que | display print queue |
| ~res | reset file attributes |
| ~resume | restart a file printing that had been on ~hold |
| ~secure | install security protection |
| ~set | set file attributes |
| ~settime | set time and data on station from master |
| ~spool | store printer output in a file |
| ~stn | add network information to MS-DOS environment |
| ~subst | network equivalent of MS-DOS subst command |
| ~unflag | unlock a resource |
| ~unspool | stop sending printer output to a disk file |
| ~ver | display the current network versions number |

MAP multi-user accounts. If you already run the package in a single user form then this has to be a big attraction of the MAPNET system. You can buy MAPNET bundled with the multi-user software at an advantageous price. Even though MAP have paid special attention to MAP accounts they haven't ignored standards like dBASE etc.. There are a set of FIX files included on one of the system disks to perform minor modifications to the following applications programs:

dBASE III Plus
RMCOBOL
Excalibur Plus
Advanced Revelation
Quality Tape
Real World
Paradox

to ensure that they work under MAPNET. All of the changes are minor and generally to do with modifying the program's response to a network error.

# D-LINK

D-Link offers two low cost networks, complete with two different operating systems – D-Link V4 and LANsmart. As the DLink V4 network software is sold bundled with the network adapters it is unlikely that anyone would want to run it with alternative hardware (although it is compatible with Novell's NE1000 card). The current version of the software V4 isn't MS-DOS V3.x/NETBIOS compatible. There is a NETBIOS and a Novell driver program available so that the PC LAN software and Novell's netware can be run using the same hardware. The LANsmart operating system is sold separately and it is both MSDOS V3.x and NETBIOS compatible. Indeed it is very much like an enhanced version of the IBM PC LAN. Clearly if you are only interested in running single user software then the D-Link V4 program should be adequate but if you want to run mult-user software then LANsmart will be needed.

# HARDWARE

D-Link offer two types of network, a medium speed 1Mbps twisted pair system and a high speed 10Mbps Ethernet/Cheapernet system. Both network cards can be used with the same operating software – only the MS-DOS device drivers have to be changed. The characteristics of the 1Mbps system are:

| | |
|---|---|
| Topology | Bus |
| Cabling | Twisted Pair |
| Speed | 1Mbps |
| Max. workstations | 32 (per segment) |
| Max. distance | 300m (1200m with repeaters) |
| Notes | Connections made with telephone connectors, easy to fit. |

The characteristics of the Ethernet system are:

| | |
|---|---|
| Topology | Bus |
| Cabling | Ethernet or Cheapernet |
| Speed | 10Mbps |
| Max. workstations | 100 Ethernet (30 Cheapernet) |
| Max. distance | 500m Ethernet (300m Cheapernet) |
| | 1000m using repeaters (990m Cheapernet) |
| Notes | Network adapter is equivalent to Novell's NE1000 card. |

D-link offer a 'bridge' capable of connecting a 1Mbps network to a 10Mbps network so making mixed systems possible.

# SOFTWARE

### DLink V4

The current release (V4) of the D-Link software is unusual in not using MS-DOS V3.x file and record locking. This is something of a disadvantage if you want to use standard multi-user software off the shelf. You can add explicit record locking to a database program by making calls to the D-link software via MS-DOS. If MS-DOS V3.x compatibility is important to your application you should buy either the LANsmart program or NETBIOS and use PC LAN software. Even though it is not compatible with MS-DOS V3.x record locking, the D-Link software has a number of advantages over other networks when it comes to running single user applications in a multi-user environment.

The major features of the D-Link software are:

☐ Resource sharing at the disk drive level.

☐ Default file locking as for MS-DOS V3.x.

☐ Extended default file locking for badly behaved single user software.

☐ Users are assigned names and devices are shared on a user rather than workstation basis.

☐ Disks larger than 32Mb can be used without partitioning.

☐ Menu driven user interface which can be installed as a TSR enabling the user to reconfigure the network at any time.

Users can log on to any station with a name, a user number and an optional password. Any machine can offer its resources for sharing without having to load a different version of the network software. The only exceptions to this are if printer spooling, time server or boot server are to be implemented when additional drivers have to be installed (a simple process).

Permission to use a device can be given at any time either by selecting the appropriate options from a menu or by giving a network command

SETDEV physical_device name /Apermission /Ppassword /
Ggroup /Suser/Xpermission /Ypermission /Zpermission

where the physical_device name is one of:

F1 = floppy 1, F2=Floppy 2, etc.
H1 = hard disk 1, H2 = hard disk 2, etc.
XDISK1 = non-standard disk 1, XDISK2=non-standard disk 2,
    etc.
P1 = first parallel port, P2 = second parallel port, etc.
M1 = first serial port, M2 = second serial port, etc.

Permission is either:

/R for read only
/W for read/write access

Permission types are:

/A for users who know the /Ppassword
/X for the /Ggroup
/Y for the individual user /Suser
/Z for every other user

For example,

SETDEV H1 /G100 /S001 /XW /YR /ZR

gives permission to use the local hard disk on a read/write basis to user 001 in group 100, read only access to group 100 and read only access to all other users. If this command looks complicated then it is worth pointing out that a D-link user would generally prefer to achieve the same result by typing SETDEV and then selecting options from the menu that was presented.

Once a device has been offered for sharing a workstation with permission to use it can connect to it using the CONNECT command,

CONNECT ms_dos_device_name /user_name/ physical_device_name permission /Ppassword

where ms_dos_device_name is one of the usual MS-DOS device names, e.g. D: LPT1 etc. that is to be connected to the remote device physical_device_name at a station that /user_name/ is logged on at. For example,

CONNECT D: /MASTER1/ H1 /W /PABC

would connect D: to the first hard disk (H1) on the workstation with user name MASTER1 using the password ABC. Once again most D-Link users would simply type CONNECT D: and then use the menus presented to make the connection.

Notice that D-Link makes use of physical device names to identify resources offered for sharing and which are referred to by MS-DOS device names at the workstation using them. This avoids the confusion of having to say 'connect drive D: to drive E:' by changing it to 'connect drive D: to H1'. Other networks use share names to achieve the same result. As D-Link is also based on the use of user names rather than workstation names it is possible to construct networks that continually change their appearance from one workstation as different users log on and off. Of course if you want to avoid this situation all you have to do is use the log on names to give each workstation a fixed name. You should at the very least ensure that servers are logged on to the network with a fixed name.

One of the interesting things about the D-Link network is that the network user interface can be made memory resident on all machines. This makes it possible to make the menu system up at any time, even while an application is running by pressing CRTL-ALT-BREAK and then selecting. This is a powerful but potentially confusing ability that is best used by the network manager in an emergency to make connections and so save files etc.

Although not MS-DOS V3.x compatible D-Link does lock files when they are opened and behaves in roughly the same manner as MS-DOS default file locking. To cope with the problem of an application that opens a file and then closes it immediately even though it is still using it D-Link provides extended locking. You can designate any file or group of files as to be treated as deferred locking files. When an application opens a deferred locking file the file is locked and remains locked until the application stops running or until the user explicitly unlocks it.

---

### TABLE 5   D-Link commands

| | |
|---|---|
| atten | send a message to users |
| connect | connect to a network device |
| cuser | create a user profile: name, group number, password |
| instimer | provide network time server |
| lockatr | set deferred locking mode |
| logoff | log off the network |
| logon | log on to the network |
| netfile | display currently open files and locks |
| netsave | save current configuration as an autoexec.bat file |
| netver | display current version |
| setdev | set access rights for devices |
| sharemod | allow files to be opened in shared mode |
| splconf | generate spooler configuration file |
| splend | signal the end of a spooled print file |
| splinst | install printer spooling server at station |
| splmode | suspends/resumes spooling server |
| splpq | display print queue |
| spltime | sets the timeout for a spooled printer |
| user | display currently logged on users |

A simple message sending facility is available that allows communication with stations that are logged on. The maximum message length is around 65 characters and there are no deferred message facilities. You can switch off message reception and review the last five messages sent. This is very much a message service to use to send information about the network status rather than office memos! For example to send a message to all users you would type

ATTN ALL, About to close down the network.

The full range of D-link commands can be seen in Table 5 but it is worth noticing that they all have equivalent menu options.

There are a number of additional software packages for D-Link. There is an on-line chat program that will allow four users to hold an on-line conference. A screen monitor that allows one workstation to view the screen of another. There is also a complete office management package that includes a full E-mail system.

**LANsmart**

LANsmart is fully compatible with both MSDOS V3.x and NETBIOS. It is very similar to the PC LAN but includes several enhancements. The main features of LANsmart are:

☐ Two types of workstation – full servers and requestors

☐ Sharing at the disk and directory level.

☐ Names for users and resources.

☐ Pop up menu to control the network.

☐ Four-user chat facility built in.

LANsmart includes the best features of D-Link V4 in an operating system that is otherwise similar to PC LAN. Workstations are configured to be either servers or requestors when the user logs in. The network software takes up less memory when configured as a requestor. The LOGON command loads the network program configured according to the details stored in a local file. The NET command will display the main menu that can then be used to offer devices for sharing, for connecting to other devices, for managing printers and for sending messages. You can also use the NET command to logon to the network if you want to go straight to the menu. The command NET /R will make the network manager memory resident and following this command pressing CTRL-ALT-BREAK causes the menu to pop-up.

Users specify a user name and password when they log on and this is the name by which the workstation is known. Resources can be assigned share names using the same format as the IBM PC LAN. That is \\user_name\resource_name. A resource can be offered for sharing using the NETSHARE command. For example,

NETSHARE APP=C:\

offers the whole of drive C: for sharing under the name APP and

NETSHARE DATA=C:\ACCOUNTS\DATA

offers C:\ACCOUNTS\DATA for sharing under the name DATA. Following these commands other users may use the resources with the CONNECT command. For example, following

CONNECT C: \\MASTER\APP

any reference to drive C: is taken to mean drive C: on the server with user name MASTER. All resources can be protected by a password and optional access rights. Only one password and access rights can be assigned to each share name but different users can share the same resource with different access rights by giving it more than one share name.

Printer spooling is fairly standard with the facility to send an end of spool signal or set a time out. The initial setup of the server allows the network manager to determine how much time is given to network tasks and how much to the concurrent user if any. In this way the performance of the server can be fine tuned.

Single line messages can be sent to users who are on line. There are no re-direction facilites. However there is a four user on-line chat facility as standard. You can also add a full E-mail module, screen monitor and support for diskless workstations as in the case of the D-Link V4 network operating system. There is also an asychronous communications module that allows several modems or serial links to be shared.

The main LANsmart commands can be seen in Table 6. As in the case of D-Link V4 it is worth saying that users generally prefer to use the extensive menus to connect to remote devices and generally configure the network.

---

### *TABLE 6   LANsmart Commands*

| | |
|---|---|
| CHAT | on-line chat with up to four users |
| CONNECT | connect to a resource |
| FILE | list files in use and their locks and close files |
| LOGON | log on to network |
| NET | log on and/or run network menu (can be memory resident) |
| NETCLOCK | set workstation clock to server's clock |
| NETPRINT | list and manipulate spool queue |
| NETSHARE | offer a device for sharing |
| SAVE | save network setup, connections etc in a batch file |
| SEND | send a one line message |
| SRVCLOCK | set up time server |
| SETLOGON | create and edit logon script |
| USER | list logged on users |

LANsmart is an excellent low cost network operating system that will run almost any multi-user application intended for use with the PC LAN. Its pop up menus make it particularly easy to use.

### SageNet

SageNet is another network produced by a software house mainly to extend its existing products to a multi-user environment. It is much more limited in its resource sharing ability than other networks and isn't MS-DOS V3.x compatible. There is a NET-BIOS module available if you want to run an alternative network operating system. SageNet has to be seen primarily as a way of running multi-user versions of Sage software but even here it shows some limitations.

## HARDWARE

SageNet is a multi-core system similar to MAPNET. All of the SageNet network adapter boards are identical and there are no distinctions between masters and remote workstations. The cabling system is based on 9-pin D type connectors and cables are supplied along with the network boards. The main characteristics of SageNet are:

| | |
|---|---|
| Topology | Bus |
| Cabling | Multi-core and 9-pin D connectors |
| Speed | 1Mbps |
| Max. workstations | 63 for single user networks |
| | 10 for multi-user applications |
| Max. distance | 200m |

## SOFTWARE

Setting up a SageNet network is very simple as the only real resource sharing provided is printer spooling. Each workstation can be given a name. All network commands are available as menu options. There are no disk servers as disks cannot be shared but you can decide to share or keep as private any printer connected to a workstation. The main features of SageNet are

☐ Workstation naming.

☐ No file sharing – files can be copied to and from remote to local devices.

☐ Printer spooling that treats the printer owner differently from the rest of the workstations.

Workstations can obtain a directory of any disk on the network but they cannot directly access any files. This completely avoids the simultaneous update problem and any other of the difficulties of file sharing but removes many of the advantages of using a network. You cannot run programs stored on a central server so each workstation has to have enough storage for all the application programs it wants to run. Data files can be shared but only by making a copy on local storage using a special network command. This isn't a great improvement on making copies on diskette and passing them around the office and has all of the attendant problems of multiple copies.

You can also copy a file back from one workstation to another so with sufficient discipline you could minimise the problem of multiple copies by always copying an updated file back to where it came from. Of course this re-introduces the problem of simultaneous update but on a small network this could be dealt with by user agreement. Strangely although you cannot access a file from a another machine without making a copy you can rename and delete files on another machine. There is a security option that will allow users to set a password protection on disks or specified directories.

The printer spooling is more standard with commands that will send an existing file to the printer or divert printer output to a spool file. However the spooling doesn't automatically extend to the local workstation connected to the printer. In other words the owner of the printer either has to explicitly create spool files and add them to the queue or stop printer spooling while the printer is used locally. This is a big disadvantage when compared with other networks.

There is also a mail facility that allows users to communicate by way of instant messages or pre-prepared files. Each user's mail is written to a specific local disk. This is a reasonable way to work but it is a little inconvenient if the workstation only has a single or even dual floppy.

SageNet is of most use when used with Sage multi-user software. As in the case of MAPNET this is an attractive proposition for anyone already using single user versions of the application software. The multi-user versions of Sage software make use of a simple re-director module to allow the sharing of a single data directory on a server. This does provide true multi-user access to the same data but you still need separate copies of the application program on each machine that runs it. This is not such a disadvantage as long as each machine on the network is reasonably powerful.

## ZeroNet OR Knowledge Net II

Zeronet (also called Knowledge Net II) is an example of a no-hardware network. Rather than add networking hardware to a PC it makes use of the serial port that nearly every PC has to provide the communication facilities needed by a network. Of course as the network hardware only determines the speed of transmission and the cabling method used there is nothing stopping Zeronet providing all of the functions that you would expect of a standard network. Indeed Zeronet is an MS-DOS V3.x compatible network and there is a NETBIOS module included. It is possible to install

Zeronet as a non-MS-DOS V3.x network and this is the version of the software described in the current manual. However any user would be well advised to stick to the MS-DOS V3.x compatible mode as this is not only more standard but also supports full printer spooling.

# HARDWARE

As the existing serial ports of the PC are used to implement Zeronet there are no network adapter cards. The network cabling connects directly to the usual 25 pin or 9-pin D type sockets at the back of the PC via an adapter. The adapter splits the signal and has two sockets for phone plugs. The actual network cabling is twisted pair and goes from machine to machine. Although the network transmission speed is low, special methods are used to try to increase the throughput of useful data as opposed to network control information which results in a claimed transfer rate of 9Kbytes per second (roughly .1Mbps). The basic characteristics of Zeronet are:

| | |
|---|---|
| Topology | Bus |
| Cabling | Twisted Pair |
| Speed | 0.1Mbps |
| Max. workstations | 10 |
| Max. distance | 300m |
| Notes | No network hardware, uses serial ports. |

# SOFTWARE

The Zeronet software is menu driven and very easy to use. Although it can be installed in a non-MS-DOS V3.x compatible mode this is not recommended. The installation menu refers to the two types of network configuration as single user (non-MS-DOS

V3.x) and multi-user (MS-DOS V3.x) and these are very accurate terms. The main characteristics of the network are:

☐ Workstations are identified by fixed user names.

☐ Disks are shared at the drive level.

☐ MS-DOS device names are used to identify devices on local and remote workstations.

☐ Connections can be made at any time using a menu driven program.

Once the cabling has been installed and tested using the LAN-TEST utility provided the Zeronet software can be installed. This is achieved using the INSTALL utility which is menu driven and can be used to modify existing configurations. At this stage the only parameters of the workstation which are established are hardware characteristics such as transmission speed and a unique node number. Following this the SETNET program can be used to set up the detailed configuration of the workstation including user name, which drives on other workstations it will be connected to, and which remote printers it will use. The user can give permission for other users to share any of the local drives or deny access. There are no passwords or partial permissions to use drives. Connections are made via the menu in terms of devices and user names. For example, a screen display

Your            Assigned to
Drives                .

D:              C: of serv1

would mean that your drive D: was connected to drive C: on the workstation that user serv1 was logged on to. Such connections and permissions can be made permanent.

A newly added feature of Zeronet is the printer spooling option. The only method provided of separating print files is the time out option but this usually works well. A new utility, SP, allows the user to examine and modify the print queue and send single line messages to any user. This program can be loaded as a memory resident pop-up menu.

Obviously there are limitations on what can be achieved without additional hardware but Zeronet is a surprisingly sophisticated and mature networking product. It would be ideal for small groups of computers reasonably close together. A particular advantage is its ability to accommodate portable computers or any PC that lacks an expansion slot for a network adapter card.

## DRNet

DRNet is different from the other networks described above in that it is not based on MS-DOS, but on a truly multi-user operating system, CDOS. DRNet is Digital Research's reply to MS-NET in much the same way that CDOS and DOS Plus are reply's to MS-DOS. Although not based on MS-DOS, DRNet is MS-DOS V3.x compatible in as much as CDOS is MS-DOS V3 compatible. In principle any program that you can run in multi-user mode under CDOS can be run on a DRNet network without any changes or trouble.

## HARDWARE

As DRNet is a general network operating system it can be configured to work on almost any network hardware, however there are a number of suppliers of complete DRNet/CDOS systems including hardware. The best known is Intelligent Micro Software Ltd. (IMS) who also produce the Commissionaire network program and a range of network utilities. Their DRNet implementation is based on an Arcnet token ring system. This is a high speed network available in two cabling versions – bus or star. Whatever the cabling system chosen the network still functions by passing a token from machine to machine. The hardware characteristics of Arcnet are:

| | |
|---|---|
| Topology | Ring but cabled as a star or a bus |
| Cabling | Coaxial |
| Speed | 2.5Mbps |
| Max. workstations | 255 |
| Max. distance | Up to 2000 feet apart |
| Notes | Mainly used for large installations. |

# SOFTWARE

The main distinguishing feature of DRNet is the way that it is based on a true multi-tasking/multi-user operating system CDOS. This should make it more efficient, more capable and more reliable. The main characteristics of DRNet are:

☐ Disk sharing at the device level.

☐ Persistent user naming with passwords.

☐ Dual logon to network and to each server.

☐ Multi-tasking/multi-user workstations.

In a DRNet network machines are designated as servers, requesters or server/requesters. The devices and directories that a server offers for sharing is determined when the machine in booted up by a configuration file. All server resources are offered for sharing unless explicitly made private by statements in the configuration file. Whole disk drives are shared but there is a facility to offer particular directories as public drives. For example, on drive C: the directory \apps\data may be offered for sharing as drive E: say.

When a requester station wants to use the network the NETON command activates the network software. Following this the user can LOGON to any servers on the network. Each workstation has a unique node number but usually the network manager will assign workstation and server names. Once logged onto a server a user can make connections to the shared devices using the NET command. For example,

NET E:=C:master

will connect the local drive E: to drive C: on the server called master. Disk drives, printers and CDOS queues can be connected in this way. Devices can be returned to a local status using the LOCAL command. For example, following

LOCAL E:

drive E: is disconnected from any server's device and returned to its local meaning. The system manager can use NET to build a set of connections to servers and then save the configuration to a file so that the connections are made when the workstation first activates the network.

The main security features of DRNet are provided by CDOS's own password protection of files etc. However a password can be set to restrict access while logging on to any particular server. DRNet also allows users to logoff or disconnect from servers. The reason for this is that each server has a maximum number of requesters that it can deal with so logging off may allow other users to access the server. A list of DRNet commands can be seen in Table 7.

CDOS allows a single machine to be used by more than one person and it can run more than one application program at a time. It does this in two ways – via virtual screens and external terminals. A virtual screen is simply a copy of the PC's standard screen, and you run one application per virtual screen and switch between them at the press of a key. The power of DRNet becomes obvious when you realise that each virtual screen and terminal connected to a PC running CDOS can make independent use of the network. This

```
TABLE 7  DRNet commands

NETON          activate network software
NETOFF         deactivate network software
LOGON          connect to a server
LOGOFF         disconnect from a server
NET            connect local to server devices
LOCAL          disconnect server devices
NAMES          display names of stations on network
NETSTAT        list status of stations on network
```

makes DRNet a mixture of network and traditional multi-user/ multi-tasking machines. Multi-user applications can be run on a single machine or spread across the network. You can also connect machines running different DR operating systems (Dos Plus, MP/M II, CP/M 2.2 or CP/NOS) on the same network. IMS have also produced software that allows a workstation running standard MS-DOS to be a requester on a DRNet system so extending the mixture of operating systems to the industry standard.

A DRNet system can run any multi-user software intended for CDOS or MS-DOS V3.x. IMS also offer the Commissionaire software that both adds features to DRNet and makes it easier to use. Commissionaire provides a security system including access logging, a personal menu of applications for each user, an E-mail service that can span networks and a diary system.

# TORUS TAPESTRY

Although Torus do make a standard Ethernet card they are more important as the producers of networking software. Tapestry II is a networking operating system, that while being expensive, does show the way forward for easy to use networking software.

Tapestry II runs under MS-DOS V3.x and is NETBIOS compatible. Although it is important that Tapestry conforms to the industry standard its innovative feature is that it is an icon based operating system. The user interface is based on graphical representation of the network resources in terms of familiar items of office equipment. For example, disk drives are shown as filing cabinets, electronic mail is dealt with in terms of in trays and out trays, diaries and calendars look like their paper equivalent, etc.

Such an easy-to-use environment is ideal for offices that have a large proportion of staff that have no previous experience of using PCs. The only problem with it is that to make use of the traditional multi-user applications you have to leave the cosy icon based screen and meet a standard PC interface. This can be traumatic! There are specially written applications packages being introduced for Tapestry and these might in the future provide a better working environment.

## CONCLUSION

There are many network hardware manufacturers that have not been mentioned in this chapter. Many produce network adapter cards and cabling systems to be used with the network software described above – mainly PC LAN, 3Com and Novell. Some provide their own network operating systems and as long as these are MS-DOS V3.x/NETBIOS compatible they are worth looking at. The most important features to consider in evaluating network operating systems are – type and efficiency of disk sharing, network naming and security, simplicity of establishing network connections and permissions. Other considerations are the range of additional multi-user applications software available to run under the network. You should find that any network software not described above will be very similar to one of the systems described.

# 7. Planning a Network

What sort of network you need depends very much on what you expect of it. At one extreme you may feel that you only really need to share peripherals and transfer data occasionally, in which case almost any network will meet your needs. On the other hand if you really want to bring the full benefits of the computer to your business it is important that the network that you choose allows you to configure it in a way that complements your natural working methods. In this chapter we examine the criteria that determine what sort of network you need and how it should be set up to play an efficient and worthwhile role in your organisation.

## NEEDS – WHY NETWORK?

If you already have a collection of individual PCs then you should be convinced of their value in speeding up and making possible operations as diverse as accounting, sales and even design. It is all too obvious (especially by this point in reading this book!) that there are benefits to be gained from joining together these existing computers in a network that allows them to communicate and share expensive peripherals. This may be obvious but unless you stop to think about your real needs and how the network will meet them you may be disappointed. Making a network work for you isn't just a matter of selecting good hardware coupled with a good network operating system. You also have to organise it and its use in much the same way that you would organise your company. As well as how to organise the physical network, you will have to consider the sort of applications software that you would like to run on it and how this will integrate with or even replace your existing methods.

It is possible to distinguish four reasons for installing a network:

☐ to share printers

☐ to share hard disk drives

☐ to share files

☐ to run multi-user software to integrate the functioning of different parts of your organisation

Although most networks are installed for a mixture of these reasons it is worth examining each one in isolation to see what this tells us about the alternatives to networking.

## SHARING PRINTERS

The cheapest dot matrix printers that you can currently buy are around the same price as the cost of installing a network on a single workstation – so sharing low quality printers isn't really a justification for networking. The only sort of printer that is worth sharing is a high cost printer that either offers high speed or high quality. In most cases this means either a laser printer, ink jet printer, pen plotter or ultra fast dot matrix printer. Even in this case there are lower cost and simpler methods of sharing printers. For example, you can buy a smart switch that will connect up to six users to the same printer for about £250. A smart switch doesn't implement spooling but it does allow users to queue requests to use the printer. You can even reduce the waiting time by adding a high speed printer buffer which will hold hundreds of pages of output on its way to the printer for about the same cost. Printer smart switches are simple to use and reliable. Their only real disadvantage is that the cabling from each machine to the smart switch and then on to the printer cannot be very long and this restricts the machines and the printers to being in the same room.

If this description sounds unduly biased in favour of networks it is worth saying that if all you want to do is to share printers then the smart switch approach is a very reasonable one. Of course the smart switch cannot be extended to provide the sort of facilities that a network can and in this sense it is a dead end.

## SHARING HARD DISKS

Although sharing a hard disk is often put forward as one of the main reasons for installing a network the current price reductions on hard disks are making this less true. A 20Mb hard disk or hard card can now be bought for as little as £200 and this is roughly comparable to the cost of putting a workstation on a network. In plain terms it is often as cheap to give each machine a hard disk as to connect it to a network. Even taking into account the pro-network arguments put forward in Chapter 1 concerning the sharing of common applications packages, 20 Mb per machine is difficult to beat!

One big advantage of sharing a single copy of any applications software is that updates and changes are easier to deal with. Instead of having to go round to each machine and install the new software the change can be made centrally.

As in the case of printers if you are thinking of installing a network just to be able to share a hard disk drive then you should think again. Supplying one drive per machine is unlikely to be much more expensive than a network and it will certainly be simpler in the long run.

# SHARING FILES

There are some applications which require the sharing of files on a one at a time basis. For example, if a team of writers are working on a manual for a product then they might work on one chapter each. As each chapter was finished it would be passed on to another author for revision. This is most easily and cheaply achieved by making a copy on floppy disk and passing the file around. File transfer by floppy disk is a very common and low cost method. It does have its disadvantages however. It is all too easy for more than one copy of a file to be circulating on floppies and keeping track of which is the current version can become very difficult. This is not to say that the method is unworkable, but it does need a self imposed discipline.

A network allows a number of people to share files without the trouble of passing floppy copies around. Its main benefit however is that it stops the proliferation of copies and versions of the same file. Each user wanting to work on the file can simply connect to the drive where it is stored and update it. In some applications this convenience is enough to justify the cost of a network.

# MULTI-USER APPLICATIONS

Multi-user applications look superficially like sharing files but the sharing goes one stage deeper. Rather than sharing data files one user at a time a multi-user application allows many users to share and modify data stored in a file at the same time. Most multi-user applications are databases or at least make use of a database. Typical examples are the keeping of a single stock control inventory which each salesman can make enquires of to discover if a product is in stock. If it is, then a logical next step would be to allow the salesman to place an order which decreases the inventory for that item. Once you start thinking in this way it's not long before you decide that it would be nice if the rest of the order processing and accounting functions could be integrated. In other words once you share data in a multi-user application the methods of sharing quickly become the functioning of the company. This is often the greatest benefit that a network can bring to an organisation.

## A NETWORK?

In any real situation any of the above reasons for implementing a network are likely to apply. If you have a network then you can share printers, disks, files and run multi-user applications. You can also engage in new forms of communication by passing E-mail and interactive messages between workstations, although this tends to be less of an advantage than you might think. Even in this computerised time people still tend to prefer paper for important messages. The benefits of a network are broad based and it is unlikely that you will be able to show a simple economic advantage to using one instead of alternative additional hardware.

## NETWORK = MAINFRAME

If you are planning to justify buying a network on the grounds of running multi-user software suitable to automate your company's activities it is worth pointing out that this is not a small undertaking. In the days before networking the only way a company would have been able to contemplate a complete computerisation of this type would be to buy a very expensive mainframe computer and as this was such a large investment they would generally employ a systems analyst and programmers to produce a tailor-made system. Employing a systems analyst and programmers is clearly not appropriate when you are installing a low cost network; or is it? The hardware costs of twenty workstations complete with networking hardware and essential software could easily be £30,000. Of course you might say that you have no intention of installing twenty workstations, and connecting up the four you have represents your total network objectives. However networks have a strange habit of spreading and growing, one workstation at a time, until everyone who might benefit from a computer has one. Being able to buy a large network station by station is indeed an advantage of networking over a one-time purchase of a large computer but it can also mean that you fall into the trap of owning a large network without preparing for it!

I am not suggesting that you need to consult a systems analyst before starting your network, but you do need to know a little of how to think like one. If you have managed to use individual PCs successfully then the chances are that you should be able to analyse your requirements and be able to specify what you need to a database programmer. A database programmer can take a standard package like dBASE, Paradox, Revelation, etc., and produce a customised system to meet your specification relatively cheaply. You may even be able to use a multi-user version of one of the packages yourself to produce the system but you shouldn't be put off from asking for professional help even if you do need to keep costs low.

## SYSTEM SELECTION

The most obvious feature to be taken into account in selecting a system is the type of hardware. As described in Chapter 2, however, this really only affects the ultimate speed of the network, the wiring pattern and type, and the software that will run on it. You can distinguish three network speeds –

☐ low speed – less than 1Mbps

☐ medium speed – between 1 and 4Mbps

☐ high speed – faster than 10Mbps

Low speed networks are only suitable for small groups of computers – no more than four to six. Medium speed networks can serve much larger groups – up to twenty or more workstations as long as the application keeps the network traffic to a reasonable level. High speed networks are usually only needed if the number of stations rises to over fifty or if the application generates a great deal of network traffic.

The question is how do you decide on the amount of network traffic that an application will generate? If most of the programs that you are running are single user, such as word processors and spreadsheets, then network traffic is likely to be light. It can be further reduced if each workstation uses a local device such as a floppy for data storage. The only types of application that have the potential to cause a great deal of network traffic are multi-user applications. Even then only activities that cause a part of a file to be transmitted are likely to be a problem. In most cases these are due to database programs scanning a file to find a record or to compile a report. Examining or modifying a single record found by way of an index generally doesn't cause excessive network traffic.

The distinction between a database operation that requires the entire file to be transmitted and one that only involves the requested record to be transmitted can be difficult to make from the outside. A good rule of thumb is that any single user database operation that seems to take a long time or spends most of its time accessing the disk will certainly increase the network traffic. In the long run this problem will be alleviated by the introduction of database servers as opposed to simple network file servers.

If you anticipate your network growing to very large proportions, over 100 workstations say, then you almost certainly need to use IBM's Token Ring network which was specifically designed for just this situation.

What can you do if you buy a network and then outgrow it? Obviously your investment in network cards is partially lost because they will have to be traded in for something better. Your biggest potential loss, however, is in the change of wiring if this is necessary. You can upgrade twisted pair installations from 1Mbps to 4Mbps without altering the wiring but in most other cases the cables would need changing. As long as you are upgrading from an MS-DOS V3.x based network to another such network then your investment in applications software should be relatively safe. For example, you can switch from IBM's PC LAN to its higher performance Token Ring LAN almost without noticing the change from the software user's point of view.

# PLANNING A NETWORK

Although the actual details of your network will depend very much on what you want to do with it there are some factors common to all network installations. The first is that, unlike the text book situation, you are very likely to already have some of the machines that you are intending to use. In this case it is worth considering the cost of upgrading all of them to a common standard. This will at least make all the requester workstations relatively interchangeable and avoid problems caused by the need to configure applications packages differently for each station. Preferably each PC on the network should have 512K minimum RAM and preferably 640K. These days RAM is so cheap that it isn't worth economising on this commodity.

If you are considering running graphics applications over the network it is also worth making sure that all the machines have the same type of graphics adapter – for example, CGA, EGA or Hercules. If this isn't possible then make a note of which machines have the highest resolution displays and mark these out as being potential 'graphics workstations'. As far as disk drives go each machine should have at least one floppy disk drive. Any with hard disks are potential file servers but unless these are AT class machines it may prove better to transplant existing hard disks into new high performance machines bought for the job. Whether or not you need an AT class machine as a file server depends very much on the amount of network traffic and the service delays that you can tolerate. One reasonable approach is to use a standard PC machine in the file server position until the need for an AT or better demonstrates itself. Then transplanting the hard disk into a new AT will improve the network and provide an additional workstation.

Most networks are capable of supporting **diskless workstations**. These are, as the name suggests, PCs without any sort of disk drive. They are started or booted by a nominated file server which also provides all their needs for disk storage. At first sight diskless workstations seem like a good idea because they should be cheaper. In practice diskless workstations are generally not cheaper than the cheapest equivalent PC clone that you can find. Indeed one of the cheapest ways of producing a diskless workstation is to buy an Amstrad or similar PC and then remove the disk drive!

There are so many advantages to having workstations with at least one floppy drive they really should be considered the minimum configuration. You can use the floppy to get the PC working at some level of usefulness even if the network is totally incapacitated. In addition the simplest way of organising network storage is to insist that any private file small enough to fit on to a floppy is indeed stored on the workstation's local floppy drive. There is the objection that the user needs to insert a boot disk to get the single disk workstation going and then has to change this boot disk for a data disk but this is a small price to pay. If this disk swapping is objectionable then an alternative is to set the disk server to remote boot any workstation as it is switched on just as if it had no disk drives. In this way the user is freed from the trouble of finding a boot disk and can insert a data disk immediately, giving the best of both approaches.

Once you have decided on the configuration of your existing workstations and what extra machines have to be bought as workstations the next step is to consider what servers are needed. The principle to keep in mind at this stage is that the network should be designed to have as much redundancy as possible. Every resource provided by a server should be duplicated and it should be duplicated in such a way that swapping from one server to another should be as transparent as possible to the users.

In theory this involves having two identical copies of each server on the network and one of the copies should be used for most of the time as a normal requester workstation. For example, if you decide that your network needs one 30Mb disk server complete with laser printer then one of the work stations should have the same configuration – a 30Mb disk and a laser printer which are almost never used. This is fine in theory but even if your budget runs to this sort of extravagance the network users would never leave such riches lying idle no matter how much they see the sense of preparing for the inevitable breakdown!

A more reasonable approach is to work out what server facilities are a must for the network to fully operate and then build in resources at other workstations which are used but provide a 'fallback' mode of operation which is acceptable. For example, if you need a 30Mb disk and laser printer server then also include in the network a second server with a hard disk of roughly the same capacity and a reasonable quality printer. If the main role of the servers is to provide applications software to the workstations and run a multi-user database then place the multi-user database on one of the servers and the applications programs on the other. This will improve the network's performance and as long as there is room on the first disk for the database and on the second disk for the applications software either can take over the other's network role.

Because each file server has a dedicated role, one as a database and one as an general applications server, users are less tempted to begin using them for other things. In the same way both printers can be used – the lower quality printer for draft copies, say. If the laser printer fails for some reason then the lower quality printer can be used to print everything at a 'better-than-nothing' level of service. Equally if the lower quality printer fails then users will not be too hard done by to have to print their drafts on the laser printer!

In other words you should try to plan your network so that each item is used and has a very definite role, but you should make sure that each device's role can be taken on by another device in addition to its original role.

As well as devices that serve the network directly you also need to include some kind of disk backup device. The need to make security copies of files stored on hard disk is obvious. In a network environment it is particularly important to make the backup operation automatic and trouble free. In principle a complete backup of each hard disk in the network should be taken at least once a day. You cannot rely on individual users to know which files should be backed up or when this should be done. In a sense this is a return to the mainframe situation where the security of shared storage is the responsibility of the computer centre, rather than the personal computer method of each being responsible for their own. Even so it is important to try to make each user take the responsibility for their private files and once again the best way of doing this is to insist that all private files are stored on a local storage device.

The best form of backup is a cartridge tape of some description. Some networks will support the sharing of tape devices but this isn't essential as the backing up of a remote disk drive can usually be accomplished by connecting to the remote disk at the station in which the tape is installed and then running the backup program as usual. Of course this involves transmitting a great deal of data over the network and it is a good idea to site the tape drive in the same machine as the largest disk drive in the network. Some tape drives cannot tolerate being interrupted by other processes running on the server and so this might mean shutting the network down while the backup is in progress. As this can take over an hour for 30Mb when using a low cost tape drive, choosing the right moment for a regular backup can be important!

In general there is no need to duplicate the tape drive in a network as long as the total hard disk capacity is large enough to allow the taking of emergency backup copies of irreplaceable files such as any shared data files. In such a situation there is no need to take backups of shared applications software as at worst this can simply be reinstalled from the master disks.

The final guiding principle is that your network plan should try, as much as possible, to follow the operational divisions of your organisation. That is, rather than just planning a network with lots of hardware freely scattered about (perhaps with the best hardware assigned according to seniority!) it is much more important to think in terms of what each workstation will be used for.

Try to assign a definite role for each server and perhaps even each workstation. For example, if you find that your funds run to installing three disk servers try to allocate them distinct roles – a database server, a general word-processing and spreadsheet server and a special applications (graphics, DTP etc.) server. In this way you will not only achieve some measure of load sharing between the servers, the users will find it easier to know which server to connect to for each task.

A very big problem is that of allocation of printers. Users tend to want to print everything on the best quality printer available, no matter what else is available. If you find your laser printer being overworked it is worth examining the proportion of its output that could be just as easily produced on a lower cost dot matrix printer! One way of making users think about which printer they are about to use is to arrange that they are automatically assigned to the lowest quality printer by default and therefore have to do something to connect to the more desirable printers.

## NETWORK INSTALLATION

The largest part of network installation is the cabling. Although you can employ a specialist firm to do this job it is well within the capabilities of a general electrician. One approach is to try a temporary installation using just two machines so that you can get over the problems posed by inserting network cards and software before you worry about permanent wiring. Also run any test software that is provided and finally install the network software according to the manual's instructions. After this, spend a day or so getting used to the basic network software. There is nothing more frustrating than starting to install the cables in an office and not knowing whether some strange network behaviour is due to a wiring problem or really is the way the network normally behaves.

If possible become familiar with the networks operation in a temporary set-up before moving on to permanent wiring. If you can show your electricians your temporary connections and the wiring details that come with your network they should have no problem installing it for you. An alternative approach is to install the cables and sockets (if any) yourself and then ask an electrician to secure the cables etc. in a professional manner. You might be tempted to do this job yourself using cable clips or even stick on cable clips and double sided tape but this usually leads to trouble in the long term.

All network cabling should be securely fixed and placed well out of harm's way. Also beware of later changes to office layout that might affect the cabling.

# CONFIGURING THE NETWORK

Configuring the network is likely to be an ongoing process as workstations and new applications are added to the network. There are, however, one or two principles to keep in mind. The first is obviously that the network should be configured in such away that applications packages work without the need for the user to do anything complicated like changing directories. Mostly this can be achieved by including appropriate autoexec.bat batch files on the boot disk for each workstation. For example, if each user is to start out in a private directory called USERxxx on drive C: where xxx is a user number or user name then the autoexec.bat file should contain –

.

.

commands that log the user onto the network
and make connection with the standard servers
CD C:\USER001

where of course the name of the directory should be different for each workstation. There is a temptation to move most of autoexec.bat log-on file to one of the servers but this should be resisted because if the server fails for any reason then the user cannot easily gain access to the network and temporarily change servers. You must think of the effect of every detail on what happens when some part of the network fails and you should always try ensure that workstations can easily join whatever part of the network is operational.

A second principle is that the ease of use and maintenance of the network is considerably improved if the network 'looks' the same from each workstation. For example, if some workstations have non-shared hard disks then connect the first disk server so that it appears as drive D: on all workstations. This means that some workstations have a drive C: but all workstations have a drive D: which refers to the same drive.

Consider the alternative situation of allocating the available lowest drive letter at each workstation to the server disk. In this case all workstations would have a drive C: but on some this would be the local hard disk drive and on others it would be the remote drive provided by the server. This is clearly confusing if users move from one station to another and it can make the job of configuring applications software for each workstation more difficult. (It is especially dangerous for the network manager or administrator who often has to check the network's operation from different workstations!)

If the network software that you are using allows names to be allocated to shared resources then similar considerations arise. In general it is probably better to allocate fixed names for server stations but ordinary workstations can be allowed to change their identity according to their user.

Ideally it should be possible to arrange for the startup procedure at each workstation to determine if the usual server is out of action due to some kind of failure and automatically make a connection to an alternative and available server. Most network software doesn't have this alternative configuration ability as a standard feature but it is usually possible to write either a batch file or a program that will achieve the desired result.

## NETWORK ADMINISTRATION

As in the case of a mainframe computer, a network needs at least one person to be in charge of its overall operation – the **network**

**administrator** or **manager**. In a network that isn't growing or developing then the role of the network administrator is to simply make backups of the server disks at regular intervals and to deal with network breakdowns. A more realistic range of administration tasks include the allocation of new network names, passwords and permissions to use the different servers. It can also involve the selection and installation of new applications packages. One particular problem for the network administrator is the way that users tend to blame the network specifically for every type of computer failure. If a file is lost, even on a local storage device, then this is likely to be a problem that is referred to the network administrator. In this sense it is better if the network administrator is also explicitly made responsible for the functioning of the entire computer system including aspects that are not specifically to do with network operation – printers, applications packages, in-dividual file loss, etc.

There are many aspects of network management that are not obvious until you actually start operations. One of the most difficult problems to solve is how to ensure that network server stations are switched on and off at the correct times. If a server station is also used as a normal workstation it is very important that the user doesn't switch it off when he or she has finished. They may have finished using the server but there may be many others who haven't! A partial solution is to provide a SHUT(down) batch file that sends messages to all users that the server is about to be switched off. If any users still want to use the server then it is up to them to send a message to the owner of the server not to switch off. This is fine but if the owner of the server is going home at the end of the day who then switches the machine off? This situation usually results in servers and even workstations being left on for long periods of time. As long as everyone is aware of the problem it can be minimised but there will always be accidents. One drastic solution to the workstation/server switch on/off problem is to employ timers that connect and disconnect the power at the start and end of the day. Whether this would work for you depends entirely on how often someone would want to use the network out of hours.

Another interesting problem for the network administrator is maintenance. Even if you have a maintenance contract for all the hardware you will find it difficult to find someone who will take responsibility for the entire network. Most often you will find that intermittent faults with any equipment are blamed on the network even if this is unreasonable. The best strategy is to try to demonstrate the fault on equipment that has been disconnected from the network – then there can be no doubt! This is not to say that true network faults never arise.

Over time the most likely problem to arise is in the cabling. Connections can degrade due to vibration, water, physical damage, corrosion, etc. The effect of a poor connection varies depending on the type of network but it can range from some of the stations logging off without any reason because the 'heartbeat pulse' (see Chapter 3) is missed or a general slowing down in network traffic due to the need for some workstations to repeatedly re-transmit data due to reception errors. The only way to be certain that a network is in good health is to use a network analyser which is a very expensive piece of hardware.

The final advice for any network administrator is to have as many contingency plans for continuing network operation during a failure as possible.

# TWO CASE STUDIES

To give you some idea of the sort of networks encountered in reality the following case studies describe two very different situations.

## REPORT WRITING

A small group of technical authors used four PCs and a number of dot matrix printers in the preparation of technical manuals and other documentation. Each of the PCs was a full function machine with 640K of RAM and a hard disk ranging from 10Mb to 40Mb. There was also a need to introduce the occasional extra machine that was on loan or test. The initial rationale for installing a network was to allow different authors to work on a document without proliferating copies of the file and to allow a single (new) laser printer to be shared. The sharing of the printer was a secondary consideration. It was also proposed to introduce a DTP/graphics workstation to enable finished documents to be produced.

As each machine had a hard disk capable of serving as local storage and no shared database was involved a medium speed network was quite sufficient. Within this class of networks a simple twisted pair cabling system offers the possibility of installing extra wall sockets and extra network cards for visiting machines to use. As no multi-user software is involved the need to be MS-DOS V3.x or PC LAN compatible was slight.

The final choice was the D-Link 1Mbps network because it supported disks over 32Mb in a single partition, but any similar network would have produced as good a system. The word processor used was WordStar V4 which is a good choice for a network because of its own independent file locking system and shareable dictionary. Additional software used occasionally included GEM, GEM Draw and GEM DeskTop Publisher and the spreadsheet Quattro. The only problem encountered was to do with running GEM on the different machines. Each one used a different graphics adapter and so each had to be provided with its own copy of GEM.

The sharing of applications software was very successful and freed a great deal of space on the lower capacity disks on the network. The biggest success was the ability to share document files without making any additional copies. This increased efficiency and reduced mistakes to the extent that it entirely justified the cost of the network. The biggest surprise was the dislike of the printer spooling. This increased the time to produce a document, especially if it contained graphics files, to the point that most users preferred the awkward task of making a direct connection to the printer using a long printer cable! Of course this was only an option because all of the machines were in a single room and reasonably close together. Another unexpected disadvantage was the adding of visiting machines. This worked well for standard PCs but a large percentage of the visiting machines were portables and these lacked the necessary expansion slots to plug the network adapter into!

The actual network configuration was homogeneous in the sense that every machine was capable of being a server or a requester as the need arose. Although this was the case, after a short time it became obvious that the largest disk on the network should be used to provide shared copies of all the applications programs in use. Notice that as each user was a fairly competent computer user the homogeneous, and hence changing, network configuration was acceptable if sometimes confusing!

In retrospect it is likely that an even slower network would have served just as well. In particular the Knowledge Net II (ZeroNet) would have probably produced the same sort of benefits and would have made the occasional addition of portable computers to the network possible. (Knowledge Net II uses the serial port instead of a network adapter and most portables have this as standard.)

**GENERAL OFFICE**
In this case study the problem is more typical of a general office network. A medium sized company (twenty employees) already had a number of PCs that were used for word processing and spreadsheet applications. A network was proposed as a way of

sharing resources for these existing tasks and introducing a sales and order processing system. At this stage it was thought that six workstations would be quite sufficient for the current and future needs of the company. The type of order processing envisaged mainly involved different departments looking at sales records and then adding details as the order was processed by them. There was a requirement to produce some status reports on outstanding orders etc. but this demand was low enough to suppose that network traffic would be also be low.

At this point in the network selection it looked as though a medium speed network might do but a higher speed network would be a safer bet. In the end a medium speed twisted pair network was chosen because of the ease of installation and low cost of the cabling system which suited the existing office building more than a Cheapernet system. The network was also chosen to be MS-DOS V3.x (PC LAN) compatible because of the need to run a multi-user database.

The initial six station network was installed while office improvement works were in progress. Although the multi-user database was not available this at least allowed users to familiarise themselves with the network and use the shared applications software from one of the servers. A single laser printer was also provided via a printer spooler. The actual network design used two identical 30Mb disk servers, one of which also provided the printer spooling. One of the servers was designated an applications server and was the default server for all the workstations. The second server was designated as a database server but at this early stage spent its time logged on to the network as a standard requester. The disk capacities of the servers were calculated so that in principle either could take over the other's function. One of the servers also had a low cost tape drive for backup built in. It was proposed that all workstations would store their private documents on local floppy disks. This avoided the difficulty of having to maintain the shared hard disk and of having to teach users about sub-directories!

Even at this early stage the network was a great success with its users and it grew to 12 workstations and an extra laser printer in two months! There were plenty of irritations and teething troubles in the early days, mainly due to users not being aware of the network's limitations. As in the case of the technical writer's network described above, the users expressed dissatisfaction about the time taken to get a printout, but this frustration was felt mainly by those users who had experienced the luxury of exclusive access to a laser printer in the pre-network days. The local storage of document files worked very well indeed and the few users who did 'discover' the storage on the server were quickly discouraged from using it by being warned that all unidentified files on the hard disk could be erased at any time!

The multi-user database took longer to complete than planned mainly because of added requirements as the popularity of the network grew. The package used was dBASE III Plus LAN version. A small consultancy was commissioned to produce dBASE programs to a specification, and this was reasonably cheap and trouble free. However when the multi-user database was delivered it was found that it was slow and tended to lock the file, making it inaccessible to all but one user. This happened often enough to be irritating.

Even in its dBASE form, the multi-user database proved invaluable. It enabled the company to process an order efficiently and without mistakes. The report generation facilities were also put to good use in directing the sales team to undersold markets. So valuable was the database, it was decided to commission a completely custom-built product. This was implemented in a high level language and designed to offer a high degree of concurrent access. Although this one program cost more than the entire network it was thought worthwhile.

Although an electronic mail option was tried for a short time it was found to be used very little. The office was small enough for everyone to be able to communicate in more traditional ways. However a modem card was added to one of the workstations and this successfully provided telex, access to public E-mail and information services and even data transfer to a new USA based office.

The overall system was a great success. In retrospect it would have been better to pay the extra and have installed a fast Cheapernet system, but even in its present form the network still gives a reasonable response time. The lesson to be learned is that a successful network tends to grow beyond its initial expected size until everyone in the organisation who might benefit from a workstation has one. Clearly estimating this figure is more important than an estimate of initial need.

# CONCLUSION

A network is the most complicated computer system many users and system designers are ever likely to work with. It is impossible to anticipate all of the problems that will arise. One fact that should always be kept in mind is that a successful network will usually grow to be bigger than your initial plan and you should always design for success.

# *SUMMARY*

■ It is difficult to justify a network in terms of device sharing alone. Usually there is a combination of benefits which make a network cost effective.

■ The biggest potential benefit of a network is in the use of a multi-user database to automate the working of the company.

■ To decide on the type of network you need an estimate of network traffic and number of workstations is required.

■ Networks should be designed so that private data is stored on local storage devices. This implies that single disk workstations are the best choice.

■ The network should be designed with sufficient spare capacity for servers to take over each other's functions. It is better to give each server a role to play in the network and not leave the additional capacity idle for adventurous users to discover.

■ If possible the network should look the same from every workstation and non-dedicated server.

■ A single member of staff should take on the role as network administrator and be responsible not only for the network but the individual machines connected to it.

■ A successful network always grows to a larger size than was first planned for. It is wise to always plan for success!

# *8.* Future Networks

Although the main interest of most PC network users will be current standards and current performance, it is always advisable to have an eye to the future. Changes in computer hardware and software tend to provide increased computing power and flexibility but there is always the danger that changing standards will leave an existing system out in the cold. It is clearly important that when deciding what sort of network to install, even if it is a very small network, that future expansion is taken into account.

The major changes in networking that are already in the pipeline are mainly due to IBM. The introduction of OS/2 and the OS/2 LAN manager are perhaps the most important of these but there are also other plans to integrate existing PC networks with mainframes. Networks are also part of a trend towards an integrated office system that includes every aspect of office functioning – telephone, fax, telex, etc.

## *OS/2 THE BIG CHANGE*

MS-DOS (PC-DOS in its IBM form) has been the standard operating system for the PC for many years and it has provided welcome stability in a turbulent market. Although entirely suitable for the original range of PCs based on the 8/16 bit 8088 microprocessor it has many weaknesses when it comes to the more up to date machines using the 16 and 32 bit 80286 and 80386. These machines have much more computing power than MS-DOS can make use of. In particular MS-DOS is still limited to 640K of memory even though the new machines can use 25 times this limit. Also MS-DOS is a single tasking operating system even though the new machines have enough power to do more than one task at a time.

Rather than enhance MS-DOS so that it makes good use of the new machines IBM have announced a new operating system OS/2. This operating system looks a lot like MS-DOS to the casual user but it is multi-tasking and it has no restriction on the amount of memory that it can use. This is an important change for the general PC user and particularly important from the point of view of networking. As emphasised in the earlier chapters of this book the biggest problem with implementing a network based on MS-DOS is that any servers really need to be running a multi-tasking operating system. Until OS/2 network manufacturers have had to either abandon MS-DOS in favour of an alternative multi-tasking operating system or add multi-tasking to MS-DOS. Using a different operating system carried with it the danger of being non-standard and adding multi-tasking to MS-DOS would produce inefficiencies. Now with OS/2 networks can be created using an industry standard operating system that is especially designed for efficient multi-tasking. Indeed once you have a multi-tasking operating system like OS/2 implementing networking software is fairly easy.

# THE OS/2 LAN MANAGER

Although there is no doubt that other network manufacturers will produce their own products to make use of OS/2 one of the most important is sure to be the OS/2 LAN manager produced jointly by

Microsoft and 3Com. This is a windows based server and network management program that provides all of the networking features that we have examined in previous chapters of this book but using OS/2 to provide the multi-tasking necessary. Using the LAN manager you can build a network supporting a mix of machines running OS/2 and MS-DOS. Clearly OS/2 has to be used on the servers but any workstations that are not offering resources to the network can use MS-DOS.

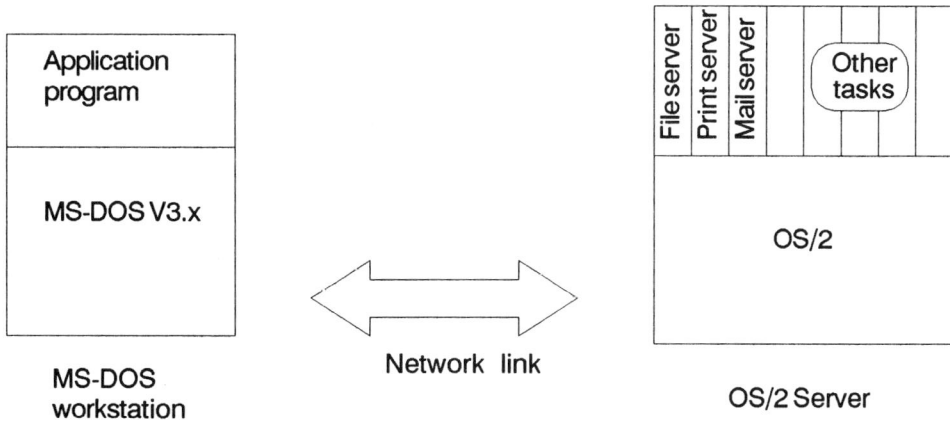

Mixed MS-DOS and OS/2 network

The OS/2 LAN manager presents a Windows interface to the user. This is IBM's preferred user interface as defined by the Systems Application Architecture (SAA) standard. Disk sharing is at the directory level and network names can be used for workstations and resources. In essence it can be best described as a WIMP implementation of the sort of network facilities provided by PC LAN or 3Com's 3+Share. Each user is associated with a logon script stored in the network servers that determines their default connections, passwords etc. This means that a user can log on at any workstation and the server will provide the same logon script thus making the network appear the same from any position. Users can also set up profiles that determine how they are connected to remote devices. There is also an auto-scheduling program that automates routine activities such as data backup and the sending of regular messages. Commands can be executed according to the time of the day, day of the week, or day of the month.

Printer spooling has been improved beyond the capabilities of the typical MS-DOS based system. Up to eight printers can service a single print queue. Printer access is controlled by permissions determined when the user logs on. Print jobs can be queued by priority, printed before and after times and custom print processors can be installed. Users are notified of print job status and the network manager is automatically notified of any problems such as the printer being out of paper or off-line.

The status reporting of print jobs to users and print status to the network manager is a special case of a more general reporting facility. The network manager can discover how many users are on the network, which files are open, the average disk response time, print queues, etc. There is also an audit trail option that can provide a detailed record of resources used. This logs both authorised access and unauthorised attempts at access, complete with the location of the workstation involved. The audit trail could also be used to bill users (see the description of Novell Netware).

An additional feature of the LAN manager is that it, in conjunction with additional software from 3Com, allows mixed networks of Apple MACs and PCs to be constructed. This not only allows the sharing of printers but the transfer of data between machines.

## APPLICATIONS SERVERS AND DISTRIBUTED APPLICATIONS

The idea of an applications server has already been briefly described in Chapter 3. The basic idea is that instead of getting the local PC workstation to do all of the work while the remote file server simply supplies the data, some of the processing should be carried out by the file server. The main advantage of this is that if the file server processes the data before transmitting it over the network then it should reduce the total amount of network traffic. For example, if a database program running in a workstation wants to search an entire database file for records that meet some criterion then in today's network this is achieved by the file server sending the entire database, record by record, to the workstation. A much better scheme is if the local workstation could simply send the request to the server and have it locate the required records and transmit only these over the network. This requires the file server to act as a database server but this is just a special case of the more general idea of an application server.

At the moment the only applications servers that are on the horizon are SQL database servers. SQL (Structured Query Language) is IBM's standard language for making queries on databases and it is set to become a widely accepted standard for single user as well as multi-user databases. An SQL database server can accept queries in SQL from remote workstations, act on them and then transmit the results back over the network. At the time of writing, the Ashton-Tate/Microsoft SQL server is still not available but it certainly figures in the future plans of many other database manufacturers. For example, Advanced Revelation, Excel, and Paradox all promise to or do support SQL. An interesting consequence of the adoption of this standard for databases is that it is possible to imagine a network where the same SQL server is used by workstations running different database programs!

The idea of an application server is itself an example of the more general idea of distributed applications. OS/2 provides a piping facility rather like the MS-DOS pipe to enable data to be transferred between programs. In MS-DOS if you piped data from one program to another a disk file was created and all the output from the first program was collected before the second program started processing it. In other words the first program has to finish before the second program starts. OS/2 has extended this facility to produce true multi-tasking pipes between processes. An OS/2 named pipe can connect processes that are running concurrently and data is passed between them as it is generated and as it is needed. Named pipes can be used not only to connect programs running in the same machine but across the network. This makes it possible to create applications that use computing power derived from workstations spread across the network. In effect this makes it possible to view the entire network as a single large computer. Although no such applications, apart from SQL servers, have been produced yet, distributed processing is obviously important for the future.

# CONNECTING TO MAINFRAMES

Even though the PC has changed the face of computing the mainframe computer is still important. Mainframe computers are much better at handling large amounts of data. A typical mainframe will have several hundred megabytes of data and possibly a number of very fast high quality printers connected to it. In this sense you can think of a mainframe as a potential high powered network server! It also has over four times the computing power of even high performance PCs and this makes it possible to run computationally demanding programs in a reasonable amount of time. Even so perhaps the most common reason for most users wanting access to a mainframe is that it exists. Many companies have central computing facilities and while a low cost network may serve the needs of a branch office or some part of their activity the mainframe holds most of their data. In this case network to mainframe communications is clearly important.

IBM have a plan to integrate all of their computing products together and allow them to be used in a single computing environment. This is an ambitious plan and it is difficult to know what the final outcome will be but it already has affected what we consider to be the standard. The dream of every computer being able to talk to every other computer, exchange data and generally co-operate is one that the computing industry and especially the user have had for many years. In many ways the network is an ideal vehicle for this matching of different standards. As all data has to be converted into a single form for transmission over the network its original and final forms can differ. If two computers can be connected on a standard network then it is a matter of software to allow them to exchange data.

IBM have chosen the their Token Ring as the one that will play this central role in harmonising their different product ranges. This means that if you are likely to want to communicate with an IBM mainframe in the future you should seriously consider buying the Token Ring network. However there is a wide range of mainframe communications hardware and software available from other network manufacturers and at the moment at least there is no reason to be panicked into buying IBM.

A standard that is likely to become increasingly important for network communication with mainframes is IBM's LU 6.2 standard. This defines the software and hardware (PU 2.1) need for two computers to communicate on equal terms (rather than as computer and terminal which is fairly easy). These standards are also known as Advanced Program-to-Program Communications or APPC. IBM's Token Ring network not only supports NETBIOS but APPC. This is a clear message that IBM intend to carry the

Token Ring forward but not PC LAN. At the moment very little software exists that uses this standard and the most common way of communicating with a mainframe is to get the PC to pretend that it is one of the standard terminals in use. There is a great deal of hardware available that will allow both the Token Ring and the PC LAN to connect to IBM mainframes and smaller systems as dumb terminals. This is clearly an under use of the capabilities of a network but it is a workable stopgap.

There are ways of connecting networks to other makes of mainframe computer but these tend to be one-off solutions rather than part of a grand strategy. Even so these one-off solutions can be very attractive. For example you can buy networking hardware and software that will allow a VAX computer to act as a server on a PC network. In this case files on the VAX appear like standard MS-DOS files. This is certainly better than the PC just acting as a dumb terminal to the mainframe!

# INTERNETWORKING

As well as connecting networks to mainframes there is also sometimes the need to connect one network to another. Perhaps two different sites both running networks need to be connected so that they appear to be one large network. Clearly the main problem here is in finding a high speed data link and this is where the big brother to the Local Area Network, the WAN or Wide Area Network has a role to play.

The combination of software and hardware that links two networks together is usually referred to as a **bridge**. Surprisingly the existing NETBIOS provides a ready made standard for such bridges. As long as the networking software only accesses the lower level function of the network via the NETBIOS then a bridge can be implemented that allows resources in one network to be referenced

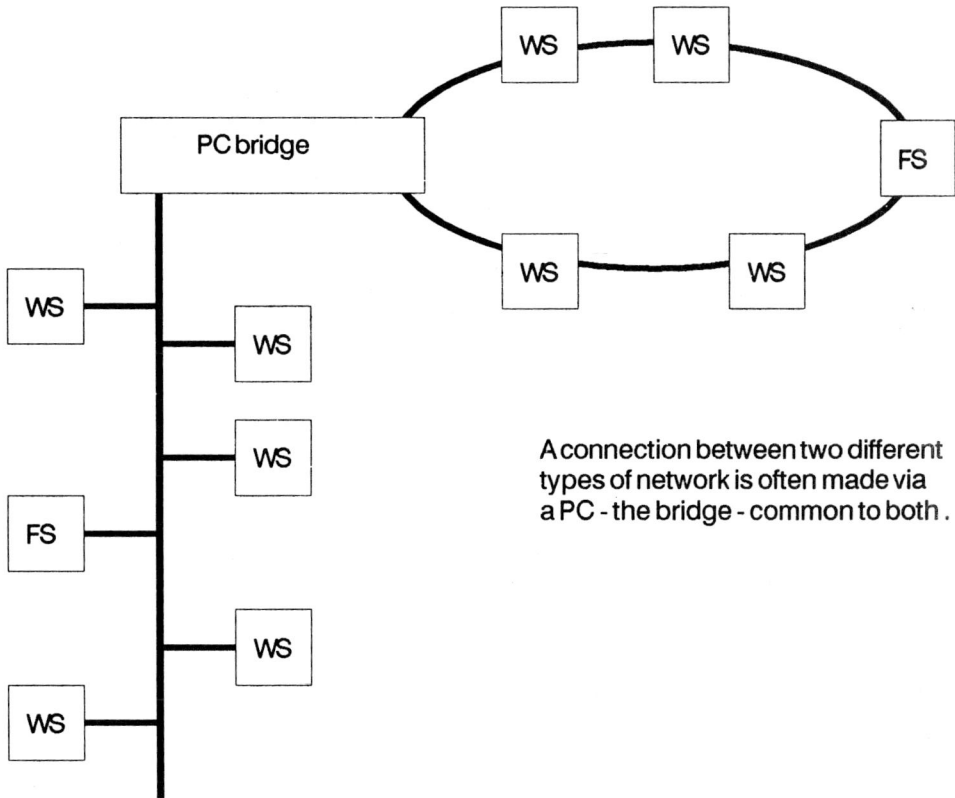

A connection between two different
types of network is often made via
a PC - the bridge - common to both .

by name from the other network. This joining by name service is
not as efficient as it should be because it would be better to give a
name that specified the network followed by the resource name.
Some networks, 3Com for example, have extended the standard
naming conventions to deal with just this problem.

If the two networks to be joined are physically close then a single
PC can be installed on both networks to act as a bridge server. In
some cases this machine has to be dedicated to the task, in others it
can be used as a standard workstation. The bridge is responsible for
any conversions needed by the two networks and for the internet-
work name service. This usually means that the two networks are
joined in a way that isn't visible to the users.

If the two networks are separated by a great distance then the problem is more difficult. Indeed some networks cannot join two systems that are unable physically to share a single PC without making the join visible to the users. One fairly standard solution to the problem is to use an X25 WAN. X25 is a standard for high speed (up to 64Kbps) long distance networks. You can either arrange for your own network to be installed (expensive) or you can use the one of the public networks. For example, you can use X25 protocols over the PSS, which is a public data network set-up by BT. The PSS is the computer equivalent of the public telephone system. There is also an international equivalent the IPSSS. You have to pay for a connection to the PSS and you pay for any data that you send over it but it can work out a lot cheaper than other

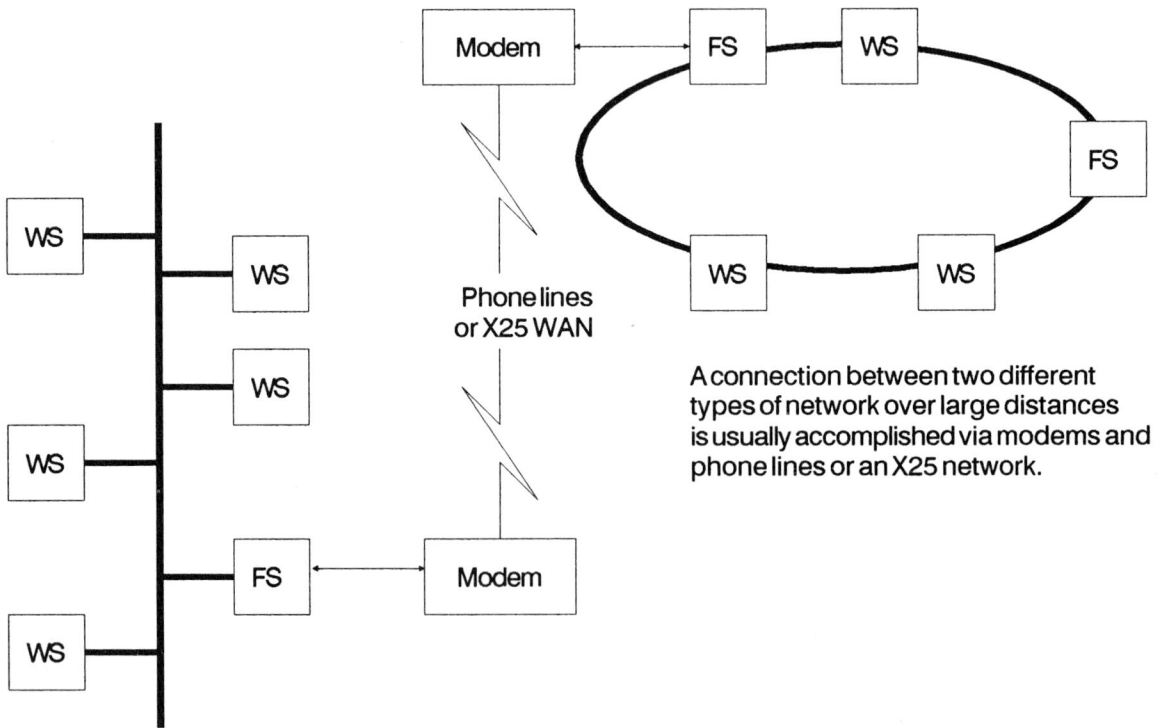

A connection between two different types of network over large distances is usually accomplished via modems and phone lines or an X25 network.

methods of transferring data. A number of networks (Novell, Torus, etc.) offer X25 hardware and software that enable PC networks to be connected to other PC networks over great distances without any noticeable join. Of course as you have to pay for data transferred over the public X25 network you might want to make it clear that a printer on a distant network is not as cheap to use as one in the same room!

If the networks that you want to connect are on the same site but not close enough to physically connect with a common PC acting as a bridge then an alternative to the X25 solution is to use a pair of high speed (synchronous) modems. Many networks do have the necessary hardware and software to use such links to join networks without any visible difference as far as users are concerned.

You can even link networks using modems over the standard telephone system but the slow transmission speed makes it difficult to cover up the fact that there are two networks involved. A better method of using such links is to simply transfer files on a batch basis. Most networks will support this sort of operation.

## MIXED MACHINE NETWORKS

There are a number of networking standards that are not machine specific. In principle adopting one of these standards will allow you to create a single network with a range of machines acting as workstations and servers and so avoid the need to set up a communications link with a mainframe or a bridge between different types of network. The only problems are that there is no clear market leader in mixed machine networks and the costs tend to be greater than a PC only network. The benefits of having different types of machine on the same LAN are not as great as you might think. Each machine will be restricted to its own range of applications programs and because each machine will use a different format for file storage data sharing is usually limited to file transfer. Two mixed machine networks worth knowing about, however, are PC-NFS and TCP/IP.

**PC-NFS** is part of SUN's Network File System which defines a standard for file transfer between different operating systems. Machines running UNIX, MS-DOS and other operating systems such as VAX VMS can all be incorporated into a single network. Only machines running true multi-tasking operating systems can act as file servers but other hardware resources can be shared freely. To accommodate differences between MS-DOS and UNIX, PC-NFS includes features such as automatic conversion between UNIX and MS-DOS style filenames.

**TCP/IP** (Transmission Control Protocol/Internet Protocol) was defined by the US Department of Defence as a standard for mixed computer networks. PC/TCP is a PC version of TCP/IP developed by FTP Software Inc. which allows PCs, VAX computers, UNIX micros, IBM mainframes or almost any Ethernet system with a TCP/IP compatible network. Data sharing is restricted to a number of well defined file transfer methods which means that a file has to be transferred to local storage before it can be used. Electronic mail, printer sharing and remote command execution are also implemented.

## THE MAC – AppleTalk

The Apple MAC has already been mentioned in the context of the new OS/2 LAN Manager and its ability to form networks that involve both PCs and MAC. The MAC is indeed one of the first non-PC machines that most networks attempt to accommodate. The reason for this is twofold. Firstly the MAC is making inroads into the business environment and it is generally recognised as one of the easiest to use of all personal computers. The second reason is that every MAC comes equipped with networking hardware and limited networking software built in. This is known as the AppleTalk network and all a user needs to create a MAC based network is some additional software to implement server stations. Many offices are finding that AppleTalk networks are a good way to use their MACs and this generates a natural pressure towards connecting PCs together.

It is obviously desirable that the two networks should work together or even that a single MAC/PC network should be used. There are some joint MAC/PC networks, for example TOPS from Sun Systems, but there are advantages to implementing a standard PC network and connecting it to the MAC network so allowing both types of machine to run the network that most suits them. Nearly all the major networks, Novell, 3Com, and Corvus for example, have hardware and software that allows a MAC network to be connected to a PC Network.

There are some people who think that if Apple carry on making inroads into the office computer market that AppleTalk might even become a more important standard for small networks. With IBM's weight behind the OS/2 LAN Manager and the Token Ring this seems unlikely at the moment.

## MAP AND TOP

In an effort to introduce an all embracing networking standard for factory and office a large number of manufacturers have got together to develop and promote the MAP and TOP standards. MAP stands for Manufacturing Automation Protocol and it is based on the IEEE 802.4 token passing network. The office component of the standard is TOP or Technical and Office Protocol. This is based on the IEEE 802.3 Ethernet protocol. The MAP and TOP protocols have identical structures in their higher levels to provide compatibility between the two types of network. In principle a MAP/TOP network can include the production process in the system of working that the network provides. Factory machines could be controlled via the network and management data and control functions could be exchanged between the MAP and TOP elements of the network. Clearly this is total computer control! The first demonstration of a MAP and TOP network was in 1985 and only time will tell if PC networks follow the standards set. However, for the moment MAP and TOP hardware and software isn't cheap and it isn't abundant.

# NETWORKS IN EDUCATION

Networking is an obvious way of organising microcomputers for school use. In this case though the main advantages are device sharing rather than any organisational principle. The ideal educational network should be cheap, allow devices to be shared with reasonable efficiency and if possible have features such as screen monitoring. However the most important feature of any educational network is that it should be a standard that is recognised and used in the outside world. Many schools took to the BBC Micro very early in the personal computer revolution and this had a low speed network, Econet, built-in in recognition of the fact that networking in a school environment was a considerable advantage. All of Acorn's products were far sighted and at the time represented the state of the art. However things have moved on and while a network of BBC Micros has an educational value they are virtually useless when it comes to skill training. Schools may still use the BBC Micro and other Acorn computers but the commercial world is very firmly PC based.

The other machine adopted by education in the early days – the Research Machines 380Z – wasn't as technically advanced as the BBC Micro but has proved a better investment. Although the original 380Z is now obsolete, Research Machines have a range of machines that are similar to the PC and support a network that is industry standard. In some ways with the number of existing 380Z CP/M based machines in education it might be that DRNET has a place. It has the ability to build networks with CP/M machines as requesters served by more powerful 286 or 386 machines running CDOS. Thus DRNET might be able to extend the useful life of these ageing machines.

It is clear that any educational network that hopes to provide skills training that is relevant to the real world has to be based on PCs. For a small device sharing system probably a low speed serial network such as ZeroNet is adequate. For something a little more ambitious either D-Link V5 with screen sharing, the Corvus network or any reasonably priced MS-DOS V3.x based network would do. It is a sad reflection on British industry that technology based on the BBC Micro isn't a commercial standard but it will be even more of a tragedy if the next generation of computer users regard the PC as an alien and unknown machine.

# SUMMARY

■ The most important change on the near horizon is the introduction of OS/2 and the OS/2 LAN manager. This promises to consolidate the MS-DOS V3.x standard but offer much improved efficiency.

■ File servers should be replaced by more efficient applications servers. The first of which is likely to be an SQL database server.

■ If you need to connect to an IBM mainframe computer now or in the future then the IBM Token Ring is the network you should choose.

■ Mainframe computers can be connected to a network by using added hardware and special software modules but the level of integration of the mainframe with the network is usually not very good.

■ Internetworking can best be achieved by using a single PC installed on both networks as a bridge.

■ The speed of data transfer is a barrier to the connecting networks that are separated by large distances. The X25 WAN in the form of the PSS allows data to be transferred at 64Kbps. Many networks provide X25 add-on cards and software.

■ MAP and TOP are alternative networking standards that promise an integrated factory/office network.

■ The AppleTalk network is the standard for MACs and might become an office standard if the MAC gains wider corporate acceptance.

■ A PC network for education is the best from the point of view of cost effective performance and relevance.

# Network Technicalities

The technicalities of networking are where many books on networking begin. It is not necessary to understand the deep underlying technology of networks to appreciate the user view. In the same way that you can choose a car without knowing about the fine details of automotive engineering you can compare what networks offer you as a user. However it does sometimes help to know where the spark plugs are and more or less what they do! In this appendix some of the details of the inner workings and standards that have been established are described. If you don't want to know about such things then you can feel free to skip reading this until a time when you do need to know.

## POINT TO POINT COMMS

If you need two computers to communicate with each other then you simply lay a cable between them. If you need three computers to communicate then three cables form a reasonable solution but four computers need 6 cables and very soon you realise that point to point connection becomes impractical.

Instead of providing a separate communications channel, in the form of a wire, between every pair of machines a more practical solution would be find a way of sharing a single physical channel that connects all the machines. This channel sharing is of course the basis of all Local Area Networks or LANs. At the hardware level the most fundamental differences between LANs are due to the connection pattern used to join machines and the method used to share the communications channel. The connection pattern is general referred to as the **topology** of the network.

# BASEBAND AND BROADBAND

Before going on to consider details of network topology and channel sharing it is worth making the distinction between two fundamental methods of transmitting data. All computer communication is in terms of messages coded as streams of zeros and ones, that is represented in **binary** form. If you can find a way of transmitting two states – zero and one – then you can transmit a message in binary. The most usual way of achieving this over short distances is

| 1 | 3 | 6 |

The number of point to point links needed increases very rapidly with the number of computers.

to use two fixed voltage levels, one to represent zero and one to represent a one. For example, the familiar RS232 serial signal uses +15V to represent zero and –15V to represent one. Thus if you were to monitor the voltage on an RS232 cable you would see it continually switching between +15V and –15V as the stream of zeros and ones was transmitted. This use of voltage levels over a cable is generally referred to as **baseband** transmission.

The second common method of sending data is usually used when greater distances are involved. Instead of using fixed voltages to represent zero and one, two different frequencies are used. The best known example of this is the modem that allows data to be transmitted over the telephone line. In this case two audio tones are used but in general any two frequencies, even those well beyond human hearing can be used. Such high frequencies are often referred to as **RF** (Radio Frequency) because they are high enough to be used to transmit radio or TV programmes. The use of frequencies to convey information is generally referred to as **broadband** transmission. In the case of the modem it is needed because phone lines cannot transmit fixed voltages only varying voltages are transmitted reliably (sometimes!). In other situations the advantage of broadband transmission is that more than one sort of communication can share the same link. For example, cable TV uses broadband transmission with each TV station allocated a different range of frequencies. At the TV set a tuner is used to determine which range of frequencies will be selected.

In a more general setting it is possible to use a signal of a particular frequency to convey information in more than one way. You can change the frequency itself as in the case of the modem using two frequencies for zero and one. This is called **FM** or Frequency Modulation. You can also use a single frequency and vary it for loudness or amplitude. This is called **AM** or Amplitude Modulation. There are also more sophisticated ways of altering the signal to convey information such as phase shift modulation but a

+15V

-15V

0 1 0 1 1 0

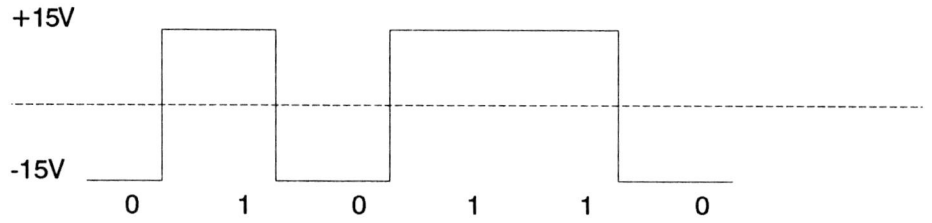

Baseband coding

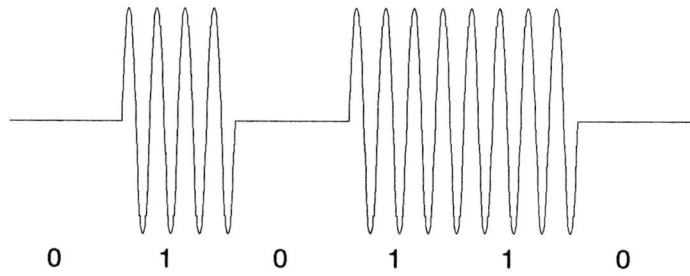

0 1 0 1 1 0

Amplitude Modulation (AM)

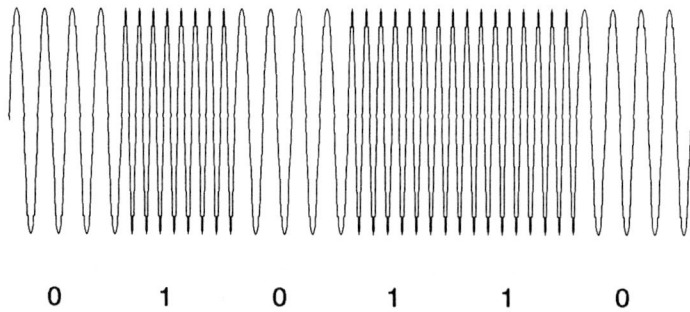

0 1 0 1 1 0

Frequency Modulation (FM)

Baseband and broadband communications

consideration of all the possibilities would take us to far from our main subject. The point to note is that baseband communications use a signal called the **carrier** and change it or **modulate** it in some way to transmit the information of interest.

You might have guessed that broadband transmission is a way of sharing a single communications link but it hasn't been used in this way to implement a LAN. In a broadband LAN all of the computers use the same range of frequencies and some other method of sharing the link has to be employed. In this sense the problems and methods of baseband and broadband networks are more or less the same. The only advantage of a broadband LAN is that the cable can be shared by other broadband communications such as cable TV, etc. The disadvantage is that you need expensive RF modems on the network adapter to convert the baseband signals that the computer generates into broadband signals that the cable transmits.

The only common PC network that uses broadband transmission is the IBM Token Ring. This uses 50.75Mhz for transmission and receives on 219MHz. It is worth pointing out that FM radio stations transmit in the 85Mhz to 105Mhz band and so the IBM Token ring can easily become a local radio station if care isn't exercised over the cabling to stop it acting as an aerial!

## *TYPES OF CABLE*

The nature of the cable that is used to make a connection between machines directly affects the maximum rate at which data can be transmitted and how immune to external noise the network is. The simplest type of cable is **twisted pair**. The close twisting of the two cables makes it fairly immune to any electrical noise that affects both cables equally. This style of cable is limited to passing signals that have frequencies of around 1Mhz which is why most networks based on twisted pairs work at 1Mbps or less. As long as such cable is kept away from major sources of electrical noise, such as mains cables, fluorescent light, etc., it works well. A higher degree of noise protection can be achieved by enclosing the entire cable in a metallic shield or screen connected to earth. Twisted pair cables with a screen are more immune to noise but they are not as good at passing high frequency signals.(due to the increased capacitance per unit length caused by the earthed screen). In short using a screened twisted pair reduces the distance that a network can be operated over.

The best cable for high speed or high frequency transmission is the familiar **coaxial** cable. In this the inner signal carrying conductor is completely surrounded by an outer earthed conductor. This acts as a shield from noise and actually aids the passage of signals due to the confining of the electric and magnetic field of the central conductor to the tube formed by the outer screen. Coaxial cables can carry signals up to 2000MHz and so they are ideally suited to LANs that work up to 10Mbps and beyond. Coaxial cables have to be mechanically intact to work – a squashed or otherwise damaged coax is likely not to carry signals well!

The ultimate in point to point communications is the **fibre optic** cable. This abandons the use of electricity in favour of pulses of light produced by a laser. The light is carried along a thin strand of transparent fibre. A laser at one end of the fibre introduces pulses of light which are naturally guided along the fibre to a detector at the far end. A fibre optic cable can carry frequencies in excess of 1000Mhz and so allow data to be transmitted typically at 500Mbps and over. Fibre optic cables are also almost totally immune to electrical noise. It is very difficult to make a tap into a fibre optic cable and so they are ideally suited to point to point communications. Fibre optics is relatively new compared to the twisted pair and coax cables but they are starting to become important for high speed links between more traditional LANs.

```
Data ──→ ┌──────────────┐        Fibre  optic
  in     │ LED          │══════════════      cable
         │ or Laser     │
         │ light source │
         └──────────────┘
              light reflects
              of the inside of
              the fibre optic cable

                                              ┌──────────┐
                                              │ Photo    │ Data ──→
                                              │ detector │  out
                                              └──────────┘
```

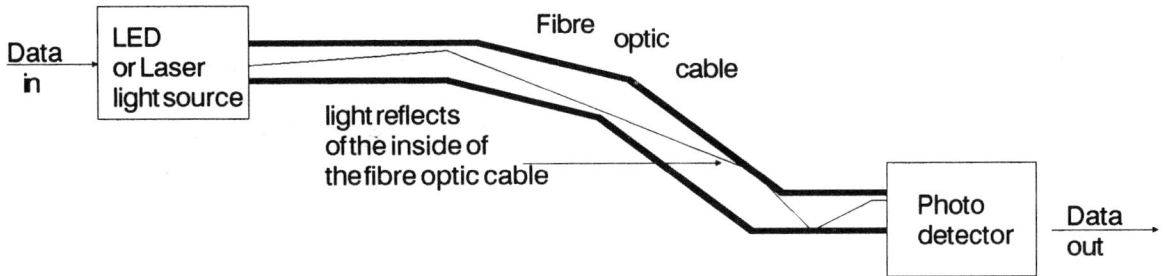

A fibre optic link

# PACKETS AND TIME DIVISION MULTIPLEXING

There are only two ways of sharing a single communications link – **frequency division multiplexing** and **time division multiplexing.** Frequency division multiplexing has already been described as a sort of spin-off from broadband transmission. A link can be shared by allocating different users specific frequency ranges to use. This method is used by the public telephone system to share long distance trunk cables between a number of callers. Important though frequency division multiplexing is in general it isn't used by LANs.

The almost universal method of sharing the LAN communications link, even in the broadband case, is by time division multiplexing. This, as its name suggests, simply works by ensuring that only one station is transmitting at a time. On a dedicated link between two computers information can be transmitted at any moment and so it can be considered as a constant stream of bits from one to another. If one of the computers has nothing to say then the link lies idle. If there is a lot to say then the message from one to another can be as long as necessary without a break. If the link is being shared then this hogging of the channel has to be avoided. This can be achieved in a natural manner if every message no matter how long it broken down into smaller chunks called **packets**. Each machine would get a turn at transmitting packets of data and in this way the channel can be shared. If the message was too long to fit into a single packet of data then multiple packets can be used and the receiving computer has the task of reassembling the packets in the same way that the transmitting computer had the job of breaking the message down into packets. Some large scale networks (PSS X25) use a special computer to do the job of making and unmaking packets of data called a **PAD** (Packet Assembler Disassembler) so that the computer can use the network without knowing anything about packets. In the case of LANs the packet assembly and disassembly is the responsibility of the network adapter card and the network software.

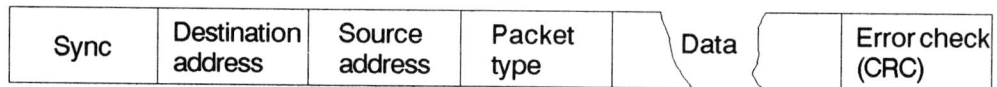

| Sync | Destination address | Source address | Packet type | Data | Error check (CRC) |
|------|---------------------|----------------|-------------|------|-------------------|

Ethernet packet

Another advantage of using packets on a network is that additional information can be incorporated into the packet to determine details such as who sent the packet, who it is intended for and data for error detection. In large networks destination information contained in the packet can be used to determine the route that a packet takes to get from one place to another. If there are alternative routes from the source to the destination then it is even possible that packets will be switched through the network to balance traffic or avoid faults. This is generally referred to as a **packet switching network** and although all LANs use packets they generally are not packet switching networks because there is usually only one route from machine A to machine B on a LAN. An example of a packet switching network is BT's PSS X25 data service (see Chapter 8).

# CSMA/CD AND TOKENS

Although packets allow many machines to send data over the same communications link the question still remains of when any particular machine is allowed to transmit. If you simply allow a free-for-all situation with stations transmitting packets of data whenever they like the result would be that very few packets got to their destination. It would be like everyone shouting their message at the same time – no-one would be able to hear anything useful. There are two ways of determining when a station can transmit:

☐ **Carrier Sense Multiple Access** or **CSMA**

☐ **Token Passing**

CSMA has been already been described in Chapter 2 as the listen before speak principle. Essentially each station checks to see if the network is quiet before starting to send a packet. It there is no one transmitting then the chances are that it is OK to send a packet of data and of course the mere sending of a packet stops the other stations from transmitting. The only problem arises if two or more stations listen, find the network quiet and start transmitting at the same time. This simultaneous transmission gives rise to a **collision** and the second part of the CSMA method is **Collision Detection** or **CD**.

As long as some way of detecting such collisions is included in the network then the colliding stations can stop their transmission and retry after waiting for a random amount of time. As long as each station waits for a random amount of time before retrying the chance of collision between the same two stations is low but of course on a heavily laden network a different collision may occur. This is of course the problem with networks based on CSMA/CD. They cannot reach their theoretical maximum data capacity because near to this limit the probability of collision increase to the point where the network spends most of its time dealing with such collisions rather than transmitting useful data. However as long as the network traffic isn't too close to its maximum capacity the efficiency is good.

There is another reason why a packet may have to be retransmitted on a CSMA/CD bus network and that is if the receiving station detects an error. If there is a electrical noise interfering with the signal it is possible for a packet to become corrupt. Every packet that is transmitted contains a item of data called the **CRC** which can be used by the receiver to detect an error. If an error is detected then the receiver can request that the packet is sent again. In a really noisy network a packet can be sent many times before it is received correctly. In other words, the effect of noise is not to introduce errors in a network but to slow the network down due to repeated re-transmission.

The alternative method uses a **token** in the form of a special packet to determine which station has the right to transmit. In this situation the token is passed from machine to machine and the machine that has possession of the token has the right to mark it as a busy token attach addressing information and data to it and so pass information on the network. Essentially only the station that receives the free token has the right to send a message on its way. After the message is sent the free token is again passed onto the next machine.

The fact that every station receives the token in turn means that each station has its chance to pass information at a given moment and there is no chance of collision. In principle the token passing network can achieve a data transfer capacity close to its theoretical limit and it has the advantage of ensuring that every machine has its turn. This makes token passing a good method of sharing a communications channel in situations where it is important that no station has to wait more than a specified amount of time. On a CSMA/CD network a station might by accident wait a long time to transmit a packet because of collision, etc., but on a token passing network each station gets its turn. Typically token passing is used in very large networks or in factory automation or monitoring.

# NETWORK TOPOLOGY

Network topology is the exact way that the physical connections between the different machine are made. It is important to notice that while the network topology influences the way cables are laid it doesn't always determine the cabling pattern that has to be used. The three main network topologies are:

☐ the **bus**

☐ the **star**

☐ the **ring**

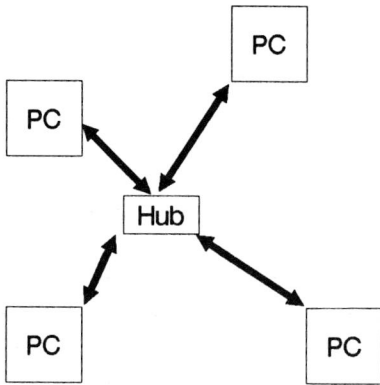

Star

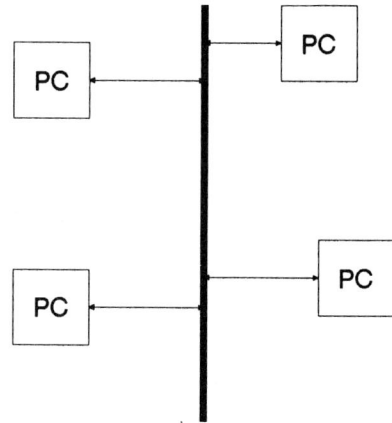

Bus

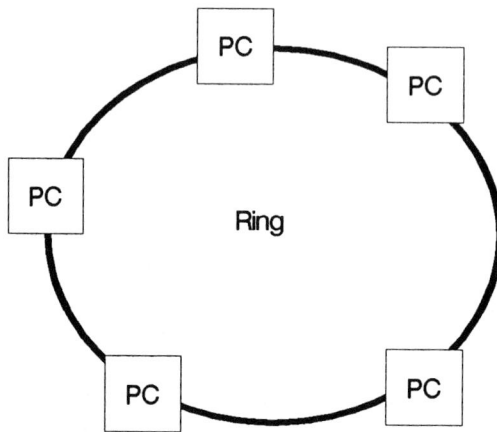

The three fundamental network topologies

In many ways the only there are only slight hardware differences between the bus and star networks and it is the ring that represents the only real alternative.

In the bus network a single cable threads its way between the machines and each one taps into the bus at a suitable point. It is clear that this arrangement allows each machine to communicate with every other machine. The star differs in that it gathers all of the taps from each machine into a single place – the **hub**. The hub is responsible for splitting the transmitted signal from a machine and ensuring that the other machine receive the same proportion of the signal. In the case of an active hub the signal is amplified so that there is no loss incurred in splitting the signal. A star network has the potential to ensure that the signal quality to every machine is the same but using an active hub brings with it the possibility of the network failing because of the loss of a single central component – the hub.

Both the bus and star topology can easily be used with CSMA/CD where as the ring topology is closely associated with token passing. Indeed the term token passing ring is more often encountered than just 'token passing' or 'ring'. If machines are connected in a ring then they receive messages and pass them on in a fixed order. This naturally defines a priority for receiving a token that can simply be circulated around the ring. The disadvantages of a ring is:

☐ The ring requires the signal to be passed on at each station. If a station fails then it is possible for the whole network to come to a halt. Obviously a great deal of attention has to be given to designing reliable station connections that will be fail safe.

Its advantages are:

☐ The signal quality is easy to control because there is only one receiver and one transmitter on each portion of the ring.

☐ There is no in-built limit to physical size of a ring, in that each workstation can boost the signal and there are no inherent time delay problems.

☐ A ring topology is suited to ultra high speed fibre optic (see later) links which are inherently point to point connections and are not suited to implementing a bus.

It is worth commenting that, although rings and token passing go hand-in-hand, it is quite possible to implement a token passing bus or star. In this case all that has to change is that order of passing or station priority has to be established by something other than the physical order of the stations. For example, each machine could keep a table indicating which machine it has to pass the free token to next.

Network topology can determine the performance of a network but it needn't be reflected in the cabling pattern actually used. For example it is often the case that a ring will be installed by collecting the wires from each machine to a central point where they are then physically connected in a ring pattern. In this case the topology is a ring but the cabling is a star.

# THE ISO/OSI MODEL

From the discussion so far you should be able to see that the range of possibilities for designing a network is quite large. If you add to the picture the way that data is organised into packets, the operating procedures for transferring data, etc., then the situation is even more complex. In an effort to try to organise our view of what the network software and hardware do and how they differ the International Standards Organisation (ISO) introduced the Open Systems Interconnection (OSI) model of network communications in terms of different levels of functioning. Each level performs a more sophisticated communications task and there is a well defined interface between each level. Notice that this model isn't a standard for networking but a framework that should be used to describe existing and proposed standards so that they can be compared.

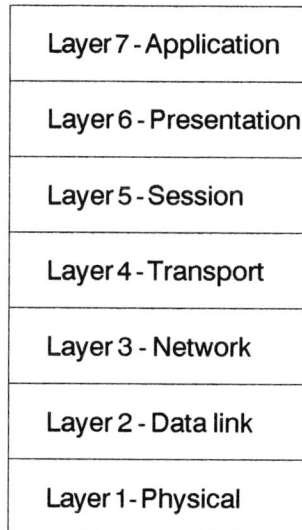

| |
|---|
| Layer 7 - Application |
| Layer 6 - Presentation |
| Layer 5 - Session |
| Layer 4 - Transport |
| Layer 3 - Network |
| Layer 2 - Data link |
| Layer 1 - Physical |

The ISO model

There are 7 levels in the model:

☐ Layer 1:Physical
  This layer defines the physical connection between the computer and the network. It includes details such as mechanical aspects of connection (cabling, etc.), signalling voltages and the networks topology, etc.

☐ Layer 2:Data Link
  This layer is primarily concerned with how packets are made up and transmitted between stations.

☐ Layer 3:Network
  This defines how packets are to be routed between networks. It also defines how status messages are to be sent to computers on the network.

☐ Layer 4:Transport
This defines the higher level communications protocols that are necessary to guarantee point to point communication.

☐ Layer 5:Session
This is an interface to the transport layer for applications. It is at this level for example that naming of stations can be defined where as the transport layer works in terms of station numbers.

☐ Layer 6:Presentation
This layer defines how applications can enter the network. It deals with data formats and representations. It is at this level that files of data first appear.

☐ Layer 7:Application
This defines that communications required for specific applications such as file transfer, electronic mail, etc.

The OSI model is often put on display in an attempt to explain networking standards but its big disadvantage is that most of the real standards, NETBIOS for example, occupy several layers. In practice it turns out that standards often find it easier to deal with layers 3, 4 and 5 together.

Something that often puzzles the budding PC networking expert is the way that the networking standards seem to be hopelessly general. In practice, as most of the earlier chapters of this book have repeatedly pointed out, the only real standards needed are NETBIOS and MS-DOS V3. But of course these are the only standards you need as long as you are restricting yourself to PC based networks. A general network can be formed of many different machines and in this context MS-DOS V3 may be irrelevant – indeed the machines probably will not be able to run it, let alone standardise on it! PC networks form only one example of the situations that networking standards try to encompass.

# THE IEEE 802 LAN STANDARDS

The most successful LAN standards to date are the IEEE's 802 LAN standards which deal with the specification of layers 1,2 and 3, i.e. physical, data link and network layers, of the ISO/OSI models. In other words, these are fairly low level standards that define the hardware characteristics, topology, etc. of the network. The standard offers three alternatives for the lowest two levels:

☐ 802.3 – defines an 10Mbps CSMA/CD bus network that is essentially the Ethernet standard.

☐ 802.4 – defines a token passing bus

☐ 802.5 – defines a token passing ring and applies to IBM token ring.

What this means in practice is that there is a well-defined standard for full 10Mbps bus networks, Ethernet, and for Token Passing Rings. The biggest gap that this leaves is the slower 1Mbps bus networks but these arc usually implemented as downgraded Ethernet systems.

As well as these essentially hardware definitions, the standard also introduces 802.2 which deals with Logical Link Control or LLC. This defines two forms of connection over the network. The first is an unacknowledged connection service that lets a network user transmit and receive information without making an agreed connection with another machine (this is best thought of as providing temporary or emergency communications link). The second is a connection-oriented protocol that provides an acknowledgement mechanism. This second type of communications service appears to the higher levels very much like a hard wired connection between machines and so it is often referred to as a **virtual circuit**.

# REAL STANDARDS

In practice there are three main networking standard set by:

☐ IBM

☐ the US Department of Defense TCP/IP

☐ the ISO

The ISO standard is the most all embracing but at the time of writing it is incomplete. The TCP/IP (Transmission Control Protocol/Internet Protocol) was defined by the US Department of Defence and it is the mostly used for mixed machine networks. However its PC implementation, PC/TCP, only allows data sharing by file transfer which is not a very powerful way of working. For the PC network the IBM standards are by far the most important.

The IBM standards were introduced with it Token ring. At layer 2 IBM has adopted the LLC Logical Link Control protocol (as has the ISO). Layers 3 to 5 are a set of proprietary communications protocols. Perhaps the most important feature of the IBM standard is the interface to the lower levels defined by the NETBIOS. At levels 7 the Server Message Block (SMB) protocol defined by Microsoft becomes important for file transfer and access between workstations and servers.

# STANDARDS AND PROGRAMMING

If you plan to write programs to run on a PC network that make use of the network environment then there is only one important standard – MS-DOS V3.x. In a multi-user environment file and record locking is provided automatically by extensions to the standard file open and close calls via interrupt 21. In addition there are a range of additional calls that perform more general network functions. In particular you can make use of the standard

NETBIOS functions using interrupt 2A sub-function 04. In the IBM PC LAN the NETBIOS can be accessed directly via interrupt 5C but this is an IBM specific feature. If a network has a NETBIOS emulation running then the 5C interrupt should work, but many provide the same range of NETBIOS functions without actually having a NETBIOS installed. In other words, if you want your programs to run on as wide a range of networks as possible you should always use the MS-DOS 2A interrupt to access the equivalent NETBIOS functions.

You can see the range of MS-DOS and NETBIOS functions that are available in Table 1. Notice that if you are only trying to implement a multi-user version of existing software then the file and byte range locking functions should be all you ever need to use.

---

### TABLE 1 MS-DOS and NETBIOS functions

**MS-DOS functions**

| Interrupt | AH | AL | Description |
|---|---|---|---|
| 21h | 3D | | Open file with sharing specified |
| | 44 | 09 | IOCTL, is device redirected? |
| | 44 | 0A | IOCTL, is handle local or remote? |
| | 44 | 0B | IOCTL, change sharing retry count |
| | 59 | | Get extended error code |
| | 5A | | Create temporary file with unique name |
| | 5B | | Create new file; fails if file name already exists |
| | 5C | 00 | Lock byte range in a file |
| | 5C | 01 | Unlock byte range in a file |
| | 5E | 00 | Get machine name |
| | 5E | 02 | Set up printer control string |
| | 5F | 02 | Get redirection list entry |
| | 5F | 03 | Redirect device to network |
| | 5F | 04 | Cancel redirection |

*(continued overleaf)*

**TABLE 1** —*continued*

**MS-DOS functions**

| Interrupt | AH | AL | Description |
|---|---|---|---|
| 2Ah | 00 | | Installation check |
| | 02 | | Set net printer mode |
| | 03 | | Get device shared status |
| | 04 | 00 | Execute NETBIOS request (error retry) |
| | 04 | 01 | Execute NETBIOS request (no error retry) |
| | 05 | 00 | Get network resource information |
| | 06 | 01 | Network print stream control |
| | 06 | 02 | Network print stream control |
| | 06 | 03 | Network print stream control |
| 2Fh | B7 | 00 | APPEND installation check |
| | B7 | 02 | APPEND version check |
| | B8 | 00 | PC LAN program installation check |
| | B8 | 03 | Get current post address |
| | B8 | 04 | Set new post address |
| | B8 | 09 | Network version check |

**NETBIOS functions**

| Code | Command | Description |
|---|---|---|
| | | **General Commands** |
| 32h | RESET | Reset local adapter status and clear name and session tables |
| 35h | CANCEL | Cancel a command |
| 33h | ADAPTER | Give a status information for a local or remote adapter |
| B3h | STATUS ADAPTER | Same as 33h, but return immediately |
| 70h | STATUS UNLINK | Drop a session with a remote computer (only applies if a call to IBMNETBOOT was made when remote computer was turned on) |

*(continued)*

**TABLE 1** — *continued*

**NETBIOS functions**

| Code | Command | Description |
|------|---------|-------------|
| | | **Name Commands** |
| 30h | ADD NAME | Add a 16-character name to a table of names |
| B0h | ADD NAME | Same as 30h, but return immediately |
| 36h | ADD GROUP | Add a 16-character name to a table of NAME names: this name cannot be used by anyone else on the network as a unique name, but can be added as a group name |
| B6h | ADD GROUP NAME | Same as 36h, but return immediately |
| 31h | DELETE | Delete a 16-character name from the NAME table of names kept in the adapter |
| B1h | DELETE NAME | Same as 31h, but return immediately |
| | | **Session Commands** |
| 10h | CALL | Open a session with a name on the network |
| 90h | CALL | Same as 10h, but return immediately |
| 11h | LISTEN | Allow sessions to be established with names specified |
| 91h | LISTEN | Same as 11h, but return immediately |
| 12h | HANG UP | Close a session with another name on the network |
| 92h | HANG UP | Same as 12h, but return immediately |
| 14h | SEND | Send data for a specified session |
| 94h | SEND | Same as 14h, but return immediately |
| 17h | CHAIN SEND | Send data for a specified session; two data buffers can be chained |
| 97h | CHAIN SEND | Same as 17h, but return immediately |

*(continued overleaf)*

**TABLE 1** —*continued*

**NETBIOS functions**

| Code | Command | Description |
|------|---------|-------------|
| | | **Session Commands** |
| 15h | RECEIVE | Receive data from a specified session |
| 95h | RECEIVE | Same as 15h, but return immediately |
| 16h | RECEIVE ANY | Receive data from anyone with whom you have a session |
| 96h | RECEIVE ANY | Same as 16h, but return immediately |
| 34h | SESSION STATUS | Receive status of all active sessions for your name |
| B4h | SESSION STATUS | Same as 34h, but return immediately |
| | | **Datagram commands** |
| 20h | SEND DATAGRAM | Send datagram to a unique name or group name |
| A0h | SEND DATAGRAM | Same as 20h, but return immediately |
| 22h | SEND BROADCAST DATAGRAM | Send a message to everyone who has issued a command to receive broadcast datagrams |
| A2h | SEND BROADCAST DATAGRAM | Same as 22h, but return immediately |
| 21h | RECEIVE DATAGRAM | Recieve a datagram message sent to you by anyone on the network |
| A1h | RECEIVE DATAGRAM | Same as 21h, but return immediately |
| 23h | RECEIVE BROADCAST DATAGRAM | Receive a message from anyone who issues broadcast datagram |
| A3h | RECEIVE BROADCAST DATAGRAM | Same as 23h, but return immediately |

# Suppliers and Contacts

**3-Com (UK) Ltd**
Goswell House
134 Peascod Street
Windsor
Berkshire
SL4 1DS
0753 868190

**Applied Knowledge Ltd**
Dean Clough Business Park
Halifax
West Yorkshire
HX3 5AX
0422 330573

**Apricot Computers plc**
Apricot House
111 Hagley Rd
Edgbaston
Birmingham
B16 8LB
021-456 1234

**Corvus Systems (U.K.) Ltd**
7 Fairmmile
Henley-on-Thames
Oxfordshire
RG9 2JR
0491 571100

**Data Translation Ltd**
The Mulberry Business Park
Wokingham
Berkshire
RG11 2QJ
0734 793838

**Digital Research (UK) Ltd.**
Oxford House
Oxford Street
Newbury
Berkshire
RG13 1JB
0635 35304

**D-Link**
Ahmos Computer Centre (ACC)
Ahmos House
23A Lyttelton Rd
London
N2 ODN
01-209 1300

**Intelligent Micro Software**
11 The Broadway
Knaphill
Woking
Surrey
GU21 2DR
04867 89085

**Locomotive Software Ltd**
Allen Court
Dorking
Surrey
RH4 1YL
0306 740606

**Madge Networks Ltd**
100 Lodge Lane
Chalfont St. Giles
Bucks
HP8 4AH
02404 5651

**MAP**
107 Windsor Rd
Oldham
OL8 1RP
061-624 5662

**NetWay Systems Ltd**
Carriage House
470 London Rd
Slough
Berkshire
SL3 8QY
0753 684707

**Novell UK Ltd**
Avon House
Sweetwell Rd
Off Longshot Lane
Bracknell
Berks
RG12 1HH
0344 860400

**The Network Resource Centre**
2 The Chapel
Royal Victoria Patriotic
    Building
Fitzhugh Grove
London
SW18 3SX
01-871 2546

**SageNet**
SageSoft plc
NEI House Regent Centre
Gosforth
Newcastle upon Tyne
NE3 3DS
091-284 7077

**Software Products International**
13 Horse Park
Pangbourne
Reading
Berkshire
RG8 7JW
07357 4081

**Torus Systems Ltd**
Science Park
Milton Rd
Cambridge
CB4 4GZ
0223 862131

**Western Digital (U.K.) Ltd**
B & W House
55 East St
Epsom
Surrey
KT17 1BP
03727 42955

# Index

Adapter card, network, 32–4
Administration, network, 191–3
Advanced Revelation, 120, 123
AM (Amplitude Modulation), 219
Amstrad, 138–9
APPC (Advanced Program-to-Program Communications), 207
Apple, 143, 204, 212–13
Apple Talk, 213
Applications servers, 73, 205–6
Apricot, 137–8
Arcnet, 172–3
AT class machines, 56, 185

Back up procedures, 187–8
Base address, 33–4
Baseband transmission, 219
BASIC (language), 125
BASIC 2 (language), 125
BBC Micro, 214
Benefits, network, 20–2, 177–8, 181–2
Binary form, 218–19
BIOS (Basic Input Output System), 110
BNC:
    series connectors, 40–1
    T adaptor, 40–1, 49
Bridge (networks link), 208
Broadband transmission, 130–1, 219, 221
Buffers (areas of memory), 116
Bus configuration, 29, 31, 229
Byte range lock, 114

Cable impedance, 48–9
Cable types, 34, 50, 51, 221–2

installation, 50–1, 189–90
Carrier signal, 221
CC:Mail, 142
CD/CA (Collision Detection and Collision Avoidance), 30, 226
CDOS (Concurrent DOS), 71–2, 91
Channel sharing, 217–18
Cheapernet cabling, 38–41, 49
CHKDSK (Check Disk sharing), 70
CIOSYS (multi-access system), 69
Client (machine), *see* Requester
Cobol (language), 125
Collisions, 30, 226
   *see also* CD/CA
Communications, inter-active, 76–7
Communications channels, 217
Communications servers, 76–7
Computer, multi-user, 22–4
Concurrency, 113, 117–18
Configuration, network, 29, 190–1
Consistency, program, 113
Copy protection, 96
Corvus:
  network, 121
  NosTalk, 76
  Omninet, 138–40
  software, 96, 142–3
CRC, 226
CSMA (Carrier Sense Multiple Access), 30, 225–6
  /CD (Collision Detection), 226

Database, operation, 180, 183
  single user, 115
Database servers, 73, 120
dBASE II, 104, 115
dBASE III, 104, 115

PLUS, 103, 104, 114, 121–2
dBASE IV, 120, 122
dBASE clones, 122
dBFast, 122–3
Deadly embrace (program problem), 88–9
Digital Research, 72
Directory level disk sharing, 63
Directory locking, 89–90
Disk servers, 66, 67, 73
Diskless workstations, 14–15
Disk-sharing checks, 70
D-Link network, 80, 158, 194
   commands table, 163
   deferred locking system, 97
   hardware, 159
   LANsmart, *see* LANsmart
   software, 160–4
   V4, 158
DMA channel, 33–4
Drive level disk sharing, 63
DRNET, 72, 172–5, 215

802 LAN standards, 233
Econet, 214
Educational uses, 214–15
Electronic mail, 19, 77, 125
E-mail, *see* Electronic mail
Emerald Bay, 120, 123
Ether Share system, 67
Ethernet/Ethernet-like networks, 31
   cabling, 35–8
   specification, 144
   Thin Cable, *see* Cheapernet cabling
Expansion cards, 33

Fibre optic cable, 222
Field locks, 119
File locks, 118–19
File servers, 68–9, 73
Files, sharing, 93–4, 180–1
Filing system integrity, 84
Flags (indicators), 86
Floppy disk drives, 185
Flushing, buffer, 116
FM (Frequency Modulation), 219
Foreground/background operation, 69
Framework I & II, 104
FTP Software Inc., 212

GEM software:
    Desktop, 104, 125
    Draw, 194
General office network (case study), 195–8
Graphics, 185

Hard disks, 12, 14, 67, 179
Hardware, choice of, 27–9
Heart-beat signals, 60, 193
High-speed networks, 31–2
Homogeneous networks, 56–7
Hub (of network), 47, 229

IBM:
    future developments, 201
    LU 6.2, 207
    main frame connections, 207–8
    OS/2, 201–3, 206
    PC DOS, 132, 201
    PC LAN, see PC LAN
    PC/XT, 32, 55

SQL, 120, 205
standards, 234
Token Ring, *see* Token Ring
IEEE standards, 213, 233
Installation, network, 189
Integrity, data, 113
Intelligent Micro Software, 172
Internetworking, 208
Interrupt level, 33–4
Intrusive tap, *see* N series connector
ISO standards, 230, 234

Knowledge Net II, *see* Zeronet

LAN (Local Area Networking), 9–12
Languages, multi-user high level, 125
LANsmart, 158–9, 164–6
commands table, 166
LLC (Logical Link Control), 233, 234
Local drives, 61, 63
Locking, 84, 86, 91–4, 96–8, 100–1, 125
Logging on/off, 60
Lotus 1–2–3, 99, 102, 104
LU 6.2, 207

MAC, Apple, 204, 212–13
Machine power, 55–6
Mail server, 19
Mainframe computers, 181
connections, 206–8
Maintenance, network, 190, 193
Mallard BASIC (language), 125
Management servers, 77–80
Managers, network, 191–3
MAP (Manufacturing Automation Protocol), 158, 213–14

MAPNET, 121, 154
  commands table, 157
  hardware, 154
  software, 155–8
Microsoft:
  MS DOS Version 3, 61, 232
  MS-NET, 91, 110, 132, 137–8
  Multiplan V3.x, 105
  OS/2 LAN Manager, 203
  redirector, 61
  Word Version 3, 105
Mixed networks, 58, 211–12
Modems, 211, 219
  servers, 76
Modulation, 220–1
MS-DOS, 66, 67, 68
  functions table, 235–8
  Version 2, 92
  Version 3.x, 61, 71, 84, 110, 232
    byte range lock, 114–15
    default file locking, 92–3, 94, 97
    file locking, 91–2
    multi-user application, 109, 112
    programs, 100–1
    standard, 234–5
MS-NET, 91, 110, 132, 137–8
Multi-core cabling, 43–5
Multiplexing, 223
Multi-tasking, 69, 71
Multi-user applications, 22–4, 109, 180–1, 197

9-pin D connector, 37, 45
N series connector, 35
Name servers, 78–9
NETBIOS (NET Basic Input Output System), 110, 112, 138, 232, 235

functions table, 235–8
Netware (network software), 27
Netware, 143, 150–1
   commands table, 152
   SFT (System Fault Tolerant), 153
Network names, 61, 64–5, 134
Network requesters, 54
Network servers, 54, 65, 66–9, 73, 77–80, 120, 186–8
Network synchronisers, 78
NosTalk, 76, 143
Novell, 121, 149
   commands table, 152
   hardware, 149
   Netware, 143, 150–1
   software, 150–3

Omninet, 137
   /1, 138, 139–40
   /4, 139
Open Access II, 124
Operating speeds, 28, 183
Operating systems, network, 53
OSI (Open Systems Interconnection) model, 230–2
OS/2, 201–2, 206
   LAN Manager, 203

Packets (information), 224–5
   switching network, 225
PAD (Packet Assembler Disassembler), 224
PAL (language), 124
Paradox Version 2, 105, 123–4
Passwords, 80
PC/AT, 55–6
PC-DOS, 132, 201
PC-LAN, 91, 110, 121, 130, 132–7, 208

commands table, 136
PC Network hardware, 130–1
PC-NFS (Network File System), 212
PC/NOS, 96, 138, 140–3
PC/TCP, 212, 234
PC/XT, 32, 55
Permissions servers, 79
Planning, network, 184–9
Posting (change writing), 124
Printer server, 16–17, 74–6
Printer sharer, 24, 178–9
Printer spooling, 16, 18, 74–6, 204
Printers, 15–17, 187, 189
Private data, sharing problems, 99
Processors, types of, 55–6
PSS, 210, 224, 225

Quattro, 105

RAM capacity, 184
Record locking, 114, 115–16
Redirector, 61
Redundancy, network, 89–90
Remote drives, 61, 63
Repeater, 37–8
Report writing (case study), 194–5
Requester functions, 54, 61
Research Machines 380Z, 214–15
Resonance, cable, 50
Resource locks, 81, 84, 86, 113
RF (Radio Frequency), 219
Ring network, 229
Roll back feature, 121
RS 232 cabling, *see* Multi-core cabling
Ryan-McFarland COBOL (language), 125

SAA (Systems Application Architecture) standard, 203
SageNet, 68, 167
   hardware, 167
   software, 167–9
Semaphores, 86, 88
Serial devices, 18
SFT (System Fault Tolerant), 153
Shadow processes, 72
Share names, 65, 134
Single-user applications, 83, 94–6, 103–6
SMB (Server Message Block), 234
Software licences, 102–3
Software parameters, 129–30
Speeds, operating, 28, 183
Spelling packages, 95
SQL (Structured Query Language), 120, 205
Star network, 47, 229
SUBST (command), 64, 99
SUN Systems, 212, 213
SuperCalc, 105–6
Suppliers addresses, 239–41
Switch, smart, 178
Symphony, 104

Tape drives, 18
Tapestry II software, 175–6
TCP/IP (Transmission Control Protocol/Internet Protocol), 212, 234
Thin-cable Ethernet, *see* Cheapernet
3 Com (UK), 143–8
   dBASE III PLUS, 121
   Ethershare system, 67
   OS/2 LAN Manager, 203
   3+ network system, 69

3+Share system, 143–8
    commands table, 148
Timeout, 75
Token passing, 226–7
Token Ring (IBM system), 45, 131, 207, 221, 234
Token ring network, 45–7
TOP (Technical and Office Protocol), 213–14
Topology (connection patterns), 218, 227, 229–30
Torus, 175
Transaction logs, 121
Transceiver, 35
Twisted pair cabling, 41–3

UNIX, 212
Update, simultaneous, 81

VAX computers, 208, 212
Virtual circuit, 233
Volkswriter Deluxe Version 2.2, 106

WAN (Wide Area Network), 208
    X25, 210–11
Windows, 91, 203
Wiring rules, 48
Wordperfect 4.2, 106
WordStar Professional 4, 106
WordStar V4, 91, 194
Workstations, diskless, 185

X25 WAN, 210–11, 224, 225

Zeronet, 121, 169, 195, 215
    hardware, 170
    software, 170–2